D0170465

SAMUEL
FRENCH

On The Waterfront

THE FINAL SHOOTING SCRIPT

ORIGINAL STORY AND SCREENPLAY
BY
BUDD SCHULBERG

SAMUEL FRENCH
HOLLYWOOD • NEW YORK

Originally published by Southern Illinois University Press
First Samuel French edition

Library of Congress Cataloging-in-Publication Data
Schulberg, Budd
On the Waterfront
Reprint. Originally published: Carbondale: Southern Illinois University Press, © 1980
Includes index.
1. On the Waterfront (Motion picture)
I. Title
PN1997.043 1988 791.43'72 88-82707
ISBN 0-573-60696-X

Photographs courtesy of Horizon Management, Inc.
Cover design by Tony Gleeson
Printed on acid free paper
Printed and bound in the United States of America

Published and distributed by
Samuel French Trade
7623 Sunset Boulevard
Hollywood, CA 90046

For Elia Kazan and
Molly Day Thacher

And for Father John, unsinkable Brownie
And those faithful rebs
Who kept getting knocked down
And getting up . . .

Contents

Acknowledgments

The editor acknowledges the assistance of Elia Kazan and Mrs. Ben Hamilton (Hampton Books) in providing illustrations for this volume.

On the Waterfront

Original Story and

Screenplay

by

Budd Schulberg

Final Shooting Script

Credits

Screenplay by Budd Schulberg; based on an original story by Mr. Schulberg and suggested by the series of Pulitzer Prize-winning articles by Malcolm Johnson; directed by Elia Kazan; produced by Sam Spiegel; a Horizon picture presented by Columbia.

Terry Malloy	Marlon Brando
Edie Doyle	Eva Marie Saint
Father Barry	Karl Malden
Johnny Friendly	Lee J. Cobb
Charley Malloy	Rod Steiger
Pop Doyle	John Hamilton
Kayo Dugan	Pat Henning
Glover	Leif Erickson
Big Mac	James Westerfield
Truck	Tony Galento
Tillio	Tami Mauriello
Barney	Abe Simon
Mott	John Heldabrand
Moose	Rudy Bond
Luke	Don Blackman
Jimmy	Arthur Keegan
J. P.	Barry Macollum
Specs	Mike O'Dowd
Gillette	Marty Balsam
Slim	Fred Gwynne
Tommy	Thomas Handley
Mrs. Collins	Anne Hegira

In the movie Mutt Murphy becomes Mott; Skins becomes Slim; Kayo Nolan becomes Kayo Dugan; and Sonny becomes Tillio.

On the Waterfront

FADE IN

EXT ESTABLISHING SHOT WATERFRONT NIGHT
Shooting toward a small building (Hoboken Yacht Club) set upon a wharf floating about twenty-five yards off shore. A long, narrow gangplank leads from the wharf to the shore, and on either side of the wharf are large ocean liners which are being unloaded by arc light. In the B.G. is the glittering New York skyline. A great liner, blazing with light, is headed down river. A ferry chugs across to Manhattan. There is a counterpoint of ships' whistles, some shrill, others hauntingly muted.

CLOSER SHOT SMALL BUILDING ON WHARF NIGHT
It is the office of the longshoremen's local for this section of waterfront. Coming along the gangplank toward the shore is an isolated figure. He is TERRY MALLOY, a wiry, jaunty, waterfront hanger-on in his late twenties. He wears a turtleneck sweater, a windbreaker and a cap. He whistles a familiar Irish song.

A SERIES OF WALKING SHOTS TERRY MALLOY
WATERFRONT NIGHT
Reaching the shore and turning away from the union office.

Passing the burned-out piers.

Turning up a waterfront tenement street lit by a dim street lamp that throws an eerie beam. He is holding something inside his jacket but we cannot see what it is.

NOTE: MAIN TITLES TO BE SUPERIMPOSED OVER THIS SERIES OF SHOTS

EXT WATERFRONT STREET NIGHT
Terry walks along until he reaches an ancient tenement where he stops, hesitates, looks up toward the top of the building, and putting his fingers to his mouth lets out a shrill, effective whistle

that echoes up the quiet street. Then he cups his hands to his mouth and shouts:

TERRY

Hey Joey! Joey Doyle!

MEDIUM SHOT TENEMENT WINDOW NIGHT
The window of a third-story room, from Terry's POV. JOEY DOYLE, a youthful, rather sensitive and clean-cut Irish boy, pokes his head out the window.

JOEY

Terry?
(then a little suspiciously)
What do you want?

REVERSE ANGLE WATERFRONT STREET NIGHT

TERRY

Hey look—
He reaches into his windbreaker in a gesture associated with drawing a gun from a shoulder holster. But instead he draws out a live racing pigeon. As he does so the bird makes an effort to escape and flaps its wings, but Terry subdues it expertly and holds it up for Joey to see.

TERRY

(somewhat uneasily)
—he's—one of yours. I recognized the band.

CLOSE ON JOEY AT WINDOW NIGHT
There is a fire escape in front of it.

JOEY

Yeah? Must be Danny-boy. I lost him in the last race.

TERRY

He followed my birds into their coop. Here, you want him?

JOEY

(cautiously)
Well I—got to watch myself these days. Know what I mean?

TERRY

I'll bring him up to your loft.

JOEY

(somewhat reassured)

I'll see you on the roof.

Joey closes the window and turns away.

EXT MEDIUM CLOSE TENEMENT ON TERRY NIGHT

Tensely, as if going through something he wishes he could avoid, Terry looks in the direction of the tenement stoop and nods. Now for the first time we see two men standing there under the doorway so that Joey was unable to see them from his window. When Terry nods they enter the tenement hallway; he takes a few steps forward so as to be out of sight from Joey's window. Then Terry raises the pigeon into the air and, inexplicably, releases it. As it wings out of sight he turns and starts up the street in the direction from which he came, walking crabwise as if trying to see the effect of what he has just done.

A soddenly drunk, one-armed longshoreman, MUTT MURPHY, staggers toward him, singing in a hoarse voice. . . .

MUTT

(as if it were a dirge)

Tippi-tippi-tim, tippi-tim,
Tippi-tippi-tan, tippi-tan. . . .

He stumbles into Terry.

Gotta dime for a crippled-up docker?

TERRY

Go on, beat it!

MUTT

A dime, Terry, a dime for a cup of coffee?

TERRY

Don't give me that coffee, you rummy. Now blow!

MUTT

Thanks for nothing, you bum.

With a certain battered dignity, Mutt moves off, picking up his song, "Tippi-tippi-tan, tippi-tan. . . ." Terry takes an anxious glance back toward the tenement.

EXT TENEMENT ROOFTOP NIGHT
In the B.G. on the far shore is the New York skyline. In the M.G. a ship is being unloaded on this side of the river. In the F.G. is a coop of racing pigeons. Joey comes out on the roof and looks around. The door from the tenement stairway creaks open and Joey turns.

JOEY

Terry?

There is no answer. Joey is surprised.

JOEY

That you, Terry?

Two men step out upon the roof, their faces hidden in shadows. Joey looks startled and retreats a few steps.

Where's Terry?

The two men (BARNEY and SPECS) advance, silently.

JOEY

(continued)

He said he'd—meet me up here.

CLOSE SHOT JOEY ROOFTOP NIGHT
Now he realizes the intentions of the two men. He looks around for some means of escape.

MEDIUM CLOSE BARNEY AND SPECS ROOFTOP NIGHT
From Joey's angle. Moving in.

MEDIUM CLOSE JOEY ROOFTOP NIGHT
He makes a wild dash for the fire escape which leads him to the roof. But when he reaches it, another goon, SLIM, appears, cutting off this escape.

LONG SHOT ROOFTOP NIGHT
Joey turns and runs along the edge of the roof, the illuminated skyline in the B.G. He disappears from view as if he has jumped off the roof.

MEDIUM SHOT LOWER ROOFTOP LEVEL NIGHT
This rooftop is one floor lower than the rooftops on either side of it, forming a trough between the two and providing no further avenue of escape for Joey. As Joey looks around desperately, Barney appears on upper level and another goon, SONNY, appears on the other. Now Joey is trapped between them. As they move forward he retreats backward toward the edge of the roof.

JOEY

(defiantly)

You want me to jump—so it looks like an accident?

The assailants close in silently. Joey gestures them on.

Come on. I'll take one of you with me.

The goons edge in still closer, poker-faced, knowing they have him.

EXT FRIENDLY BAR NIGHT

An old-fashioned corner saloon with swinging doors. Standing on the corner, flanked by a goon aptly named the TRUCK is CHARLEY, THE GENT, Terry's older brother, rather handsome if a little too smooth, in his late thirties, a snappy dresser in his camel hair coat and snap brim hat. He is quick-witted and affable, more politician than mobster. Terry enters to him.

CHARLEY

(gently)

How goes?

TERRY

(tightly)

He's on the roof.

CHARLEY

The pigeon?

TERRY

(resentfully)

Like you said. It worked.

TRUCK

(to Terry, tapping his own temple)

That brother of yours is thinkin' alla time. . . .

TERRY

(tense)

All the time.

There is a short, shrill, almost human cry of a boat whistle. It changes slightly in pitch and we are hearing an actual cry.

CLOSE SHOT BODY OF JOEY

Hurtling off roof, with a bloodcurdling shriek.

INT CLOSE SHOT WOMAN AT WINDOW (MRS. COLLINS)

She screams.

EXT FRIENDLY BAR FAVORING TERRY NIGHT
Worried as he begins to wonder what has happened.

TRUCK

I'm afraid somebody fell off a roof.

Terry stares at him. Longshoremen come running out of the bar toward the sound of the scream. Terry has to struggle not to be carried along with them. He works his way toward Charley, standing on the curb with Truck, calmly watching the Friendly Bar customers excitedly running past him. (Calls and commotion in the distance O.S.)

TRUCK

He thought he was gonna sing for the Crime Commission. He won't.

Truck winks at Charley significantly. Terry catches the meaning and is horrified.

TERRY

(accusingly)

You said they was only going to talk to him.

CHARLEY

That was the idea.

TERRY

I thought they'd talk to him. Try to get him to dummy up.

CHARLEY

Maybe he gave them an argument.

TERRY

I figured the worst they'd do is work him over a little.

CHARLEY

He probably gave 'em an argument.

TRUCK

(almost primly)

He's been giving our boss a lot of trouble.

TERRY

He wasn't a bad little fella, that Joey.

CHARLEY

No he wasn't.

TRUCK

Except for his mouth.

CHARLEY

Talkative.

TERRY

(muttering to himself)

Wasn't a bad little fella. . . .

TRUCK

(chuckling)

Maybe he could sing, but he couldn't fly.

Terry looks at Truck, stricken.

CHARLEY

(sympathetically, nodding toward bar)

Come on, kid, I'll buy you a drink.

TERRY

(bewildered)

—In a minute.

Charley looks at him, slightly concerned, and goes in with Truck. Terry watches the longshoremen hurrying past him, in the direction of—

EXT LANDING BELOW TENEMENT ROOF NIGHT

Forming a circle around Joey are KAYO NOLAN, a hard little nut of a man; TOMMY COLLINS, a young longshoreman friend of Joey's; LUKE, a giant Negro; MOOSE, a good-natured, hulking longshoreman; and others. The shot favors POP DOYLE, a short, stocky man with a small potbelly.

POP

(to someone running up)

I kept tellin' him: don't say nothin', keep quiet, you'll live longer.

POLICE SERGEANT

(to another cop)

Tell the ambulance to hurry.

SHOT OF ONLOOKERS ROOFTOP NIGHT

Including a hard-faced longshoreman, a careworn woman in her middle thirties (Mrs. Collins) and Mutt.

LONGSHOREMAN
He ain't gonna need no ambulance.

FATHER BARRY, a lean, tough, West Side priest, climbs a wooden fence and approaches crowd.

FATHER BARRY
(roughly)
One side. Le'me through!

MEDIUM SHOT MRS. COLLINS, MUTT ROOFTOP NIGHT

MRS. COLLINS
(to Father Barry as he passes)
Same thing they did to my Andy five years ago.

CLOSE ON BODY OF JOEY TENEMENT LANDING NIGHT
Father Barry prays. A police sergeant turns to Pop.

SERGEANT
You're Pop Doyle, aren't you, the boy's father?

POP
(angrily)
That's right.

SERGEANT
He fell over backward from the roof—like he was pushed. Any ideas?

POP
(aggressively)
None.

MRS. COLLINS
(coming forward)
He was the one longshoreman with guts enough to talk to them crime investigators. Everybody knows that.

POP
(wheeling angrily and pushing her away)
Who asked you. Shut your trap. If Joey'd taken that advice he wouldn't be—
(starts to crack up)

MRS. COLLINS

(protesting)

Everybody know that . . . ?

POP

I said shut up!

SERGEANT

Look, I'm an honest cop. Give me some leads and I'll—

Pop stands silently, choked with grief.

KAYO NOLAN

Listen—don't bother him. Right, Moose?

MOOSE

(nodding)

One thing I learned—all my life on the waterfront—don't ask no questions—don't answer no questions. Unless you. . . .

(looks at the body and stops)

LUKE

(reverently)

He was all heart, that boy. Enough guts for a regiment.

POP

(in a bitter rage)

Guts—I'm sick of guts. He gets a book in the pistol local and right away he's gonna be a hero. Gonna push the mob off the dock singlehanded. . . .

FATHER BARRY

(comfortingly)

Take it easy, Pop. I know it's rough but time and faith are great healers. . . .

CLOSE ON EDIE TENEMENT LANDING NIGHT

Joey's sister, a fresh-faced, sensitive young Irish girl who has been kneeling over the body. She looks up and around at the Father in bitter grief.

EDIE

Time and faith . . . My brother's dead and you stand there talking drivel about time and faith.

FATHER BARRY

(taken aback)

Why Edie, I—

EDIE

(plunging on)

How could anyone do this to Joey. The best in the neighborhood—everybody said it, not only me. Who'd want to harm Joey? Tell me—who?—who?

FATHER BARRY

(embarrassed)

I wish I knew, Edie, but—

(starts to turn away as if appealing to the others)

EDIE

Don't turn away! Look at it! You're in this too—don't you see, don't you *see?* You're in this too, Father.

FATHER BARRY

(defensively, sincerely)

Edie, I do what I can. I'm in the church when you need me.

EDIE

(bitingly)

"In the church when you need me." Was there ever a saint who hid in the Church?

She turns from him angrily, toward the covered form of Joey.

CLOSE SHOT FATHER BARRY

Father Barry stands there jolted and troubled.

MRS. COLLINS

(moves in to him)

Forgive her, Father. Them two was as close as twins.

Father Barry nods. Thinking hard.

MRS. COLLINS

(continued)

Who ever was in on this'll burn in hell until kingdom come. . . .

DISSOLVE

INT FRIENDLY BAR NIGHT

The atmosphere is the sharpest possible contrast to the scene above.

It is a rough waterfront bar full of half-gassed longshoremen and pistol boys. They are all watching a fight on TV above the bar, and there is much hoarse laughter and ad lib jokes at the fight. The only one not watching is Terry, who sits at a table by himself staring at a half-finished glass of beer. Mutt is wandering around in the B.G.

VOICE

(O.S.)

Hey, Terry, Riley's makin' a bum outa that Solari—

Terry looks off and sees—

MEDIUM SHOT BARNEY AND SPECS AT BAR NIGHT

Unconcernedly drinking and enjoying the fight.

SPECS

Come on over and have a shot.

Still disturbed and preoccupied, Terry shakes his head and goes on through the bar toward the back room. Others call to him but he keeps going.

INT BACK ROOM OF BAR NIGHT

A partition separates this room from the main bar, and a small corner of the bar extends through the partition. On the wall are old fight posters and some pictures of fighters, ball players and horses. At a table, flanked by Charley and a tall, muscular bodyguard, Sonny, is JOHNNY FRIENDLY. He is not tough in a conventional way, but with a sinister intent, a humorless sense of domination that is really dangerous. The boxing match can be seen on a smaller TV set.

JOHNNY FRIENDLY

Turn if off. Them clowns can't fight. There's nobody tough anymore.

JOCKO, the bartender, pokes his head through the archway behind the bar.

JOCKO

Hey, boss, Packy wants another one on the cuff?

JOHNNY

(with a generous wave of his hand)

Give it to him!

As Johnny finishes off a bottle of beer, BIG MAC, the bullnecked hiring boss, comes up to the table with a thick roll of bills.

BIG MAC

Here's the cut from the shape-up. Eight hundred and ninety-one men at three bucks a head makes—

(puts on glasses, incongruous on his beefy face)

—twenty-six seventy-three.

JOHNNY

(to Charley)

Here, you count it. Countin' makes me sleepy.

Terry enters during the above and sits at the bar, brooding. Johnny is glad to see him.

JOHNNY

(continued)

Hya, slugger, how they hangin'?

TERRY

(subdued)

So-so, Johnny.

JOHNNY

(pantomiming, defending against blows)

Don't hit me, now, don't hit me!

BIG MAC

We got a banana boat at forty-six tomorra. If we pull a walkout it might be a few bucks from the shippers. Them bananas go bad in a hurry.

JOHNNY

We'll ask ten G.

(looks around)

Where's Morgan? Where's that big banker of mine?

As Johnny talks he holds on to Terry, and fondles him casually. MORGAN, a big-eared, large-nosed little weasel of a man, pokes his head in the door as if he were waiting just outside.

MORGAN

Right here, boss.

JOHNNY

(mockingly—Morgan is a sort of court jester)

Well, J.P., how's business?

J.P.

Havin' trouble with Kelly again, boss. He won't take no loans and Big Mac puts him to work anyway.

BIG MAC

(shouting at J.P.)

He's my wife's nephew.

J.P.

(right back at Big Mac)

But he don't take no loans.

BIG MAC

I got to give him work. She'd murda me. . . .

J.P.

(shakes his head)

That's why I stay single.

(turns to Johnny)

Here's the interest on the day, boss. Five thirty two.

JOHNNY

(taking it from him and handing it to Sonny)

Count it.

Now Sonny and Charley are both counting. SKINS, another runner for the mob, a nervous, pasty-faced man, enters.

JOHNNY

(continued)

Hey, Skins—

(as Skins approaches Johnny lowers his voice)

—get away with that sheet metal all right?

SKINS

Easy, that new checker faked the receipt. Here it is, boss.

(offers receipt)

JOHNNY

Stow the receipt. I'll take the cash.

SKINS

(producing another roll of bills)

Forty-five bills.

JOHNNY

(to Terry, sulking at the bar)

Hey, Terry, front and center.

Terry comes over reluctantly and Johnny hands him the bills.

JOHNNY

(continued)

Count this.

TERRY

Aw, you know I don't like to count, Johnny.

JOHNNY

It's good for you. Develops your mind.

SKINS

What mind?

He starts to laugh but Johnny stops him with a look.

JOHNNY

Shut up. I like the kid.

(tweaks Terry's cheek fondly)

Remember the night he took Farella at St. Nick's, Charley. We won a bundle. Real tough. A big try.

TERRY

(stops counting and taps his nose proudly)

Not a dent.

(tweaks his nose)

Perfect.

JOHNNY

(laughs, rubs Terry's head)

My favorite little cousin.

TERRY

(disconcerted as he tries to count)

Thirty-six—sev—aah I lost the count.

JOHNNY

(tolerantly)

OK—skip it, Einstein. How come you never got no education like the rest of us?

BIG MAC

(good-naturedly)

Only arithmetic he got was hearing the referee count up to ten.

TERRY

(hot-tempered, starting to attack Big Mac)

Now listen, Mac—

Johnny laughs and pulls Terry back.

JOHNNY

(amused)

What gives with our boy tonight, Charley? He ain't himself.

CHARLEY

(as if Terry were not there)

The Joey Doyle thing. You know how he is. Things like that—he exaggerates them. Too much Marquis of Queensbury. It softens 'em up.

JOHNNY

(taking the money from Sonny, Skins and J.P. and dealing out some bills to each of them as if the money were cards, while Charley goes on counting)

Listen kid, I'm a soft touch too. Ask any rummy on the dock if I'm not good for a fin any time they put the arm on me.

(then more harshly)

But my old lady raised us ten kids on a stinkin' watchman's pension. When I was sixteen I had to beg for work in the hold. I didn't work my way up out of there for nuthin'.

TERRY

(sorry to have aroused Johnny—who speaks loud and with frightening force when stung)

I know, Johnny, I know. . . .

JOHNNY

Takin' over this local, you know it took a little doin'. Some

pretty tough fellas were in the way. They left me this—
(suddenly holds up chin to show a long ugly scar on neck)
—to remember them by.

CHARLEY
(admiringly)
When he got up and chased them they thought it was a dead man coming after them.

JOHNNY
(to Terry)
I know what's eatin' you, kid. But I got two thousand dues-payin' members in my local—that's seventy-two thousand a year *legitimate* and when each one of 'em puts in a couple of bucks a day to make sure they work steady—well, you figure it out. And that's just for openers. We got the fattest piers in the fattest harbor in the world. Everything that moves in and out—we take our cut.

CHARLEY
Why shouldn't we? If we c'n get it we're entitled to it.

JOHNNY
(nods)
We ain't robbin' pennies from beggars. We cuttin' ourselves in for five-six million a year just on our half a dozen piers—a drop in the bucket compared to the traffic in the harbor. But a mighty sweet little drop, eh, Charley?

CHARLEY
(wisely)
It'll do.

JOHNNY
So look, kid, you don't think we c'n afford to be boxed out of a deal like this—a deal I sweated and bled for—on account of one lousy little cheese-eater, that Doyle bum, who thought he c'd go squealin' to the Crime Commission? Do you?

Terry is uncomfortably silent. Johnny raises his voice.
Do you?

TERRY

Well, no, Johnny, I just thought I should've been told if—

CHARLEY

(handing back the money)

I make it twenty-six *twenty*-three. You're fifty short, Skins.

JOHNNY

(turning darkly on Skins)

Gimme.

SKINS

(frightened)

I—I musta counted wrong, boss, I—

JOHNNY

Gimme.

He reaches over and takes money out of Skins's pockets, stripping him.

JOHNNY

(continued)

You come from Green Point? Go back to Green Point. You don't work here no more.

(impulsively he hands the bill to Terry—smiling)

Here, kid, here's half a bill. Go get your load on.

TERRY

(still troubled)

Naw, thanks, Johnny, I don't want it, I—

JOHNNY

(roughly)

Go on—a little present from your Uncle Johnny.

(He pushes the bill into the breast pocket of Terry's jacket.)

(then turns to Big Mac)

And Mac, tomorra mornin' when you shape the men put Terry in the loft. Number one. Every day.

(to Terry)

Nice easy work. Check in and goof off on the coffee bags. O.K.?

TERRY

(frowning)

Thanks, Johnny. . . .

CHARLEY

(a kind of warning)

You got a real friend here, kid. Don't forget it.

JOHNNY

(smiling)

Why should he forget it?

As Terry turns away, toward the bar,

DISSOLVE

EXT TENEMENT ROOF DAYBREAK

Terry, darkly troubled, is watching the pigeons he has just fed when JIMMY CONNERS, a freckle-faced fourteen-year-old boy, approaches along the same stretch of roof seen in the mugging of Joey.

JIMMY

Hi!

Terry turns around startled, as Jimmy comes climbing up out of the trough where Joey was trapped.

I was just gonna feed 'em, Terry.

TERRY

's all right, kid, I took care of 'em myself this morning.

JIMMY

Boy, you must've been up early.

TERRY

(as if he hardly slept)

Yeah, yeah, I was awake anyway so I figured—

(gestures toward feeding pigeons; then with admiration)

They got it made. Eat all they want—fly around like crazy—sleep side by side—and raise gobs of squabs.

O.S. or in B.G. a ship coming into port sounds its whistle, bringing him back to reality.

I better get over there.

(O.S. sound of ship whistle again. Terry answers the ship irritably)

O.K., O.K., I'm coming.
(starts off)
Don't spill no water on the floor now. I don't want them birds to catch cold.

Jimmy signals the Golden Warrior salute—the first two fingers raised together. Terry answers with the same salute as he goes off, disturbed.

DISSOLVE

EXT LONG SHOT PIER DAY
Some three hundred men are standing around, men of all sizes and ages, some in dungarees, some in baggy denims, wearing battered windbreakers or service discards, and either caps or woolen pullovers. A sprinkling of Negroes. A ship is berthing in the B.G. The mood is somber and restless.

CLOSER SHOTS LONGSHOREMEN
Muttering to each other.

AD LIBS
He was a good boy, the Doyle kid.
Sure he was, that's why he got it in the head.
Couldn't learn to keep his mouth shut.

MEDIUM CLOSE ON TERRY
With his chum, JACKIE, as another pal, CHICK, comes up. Terry looks around as if trying to hear what the men are muttering behind him.

CHICK
(to Jackie but really to Terry)
Hey Jackie, what d'ya think of this privileged character? Don't have to shape up no more. Got himself a soft touch up in the loft.
(mimics sound of snoring)

TERRY
(defensively)
Who told you that?

CHICK
(winks at Jackie)
Waterfront Western Union.
(business of putting his hand to his mouth)

Terry looks around at the restless men again.

JACKIE

You're doin' lovely, Terry, very lovely.

TERRY

(hotly)

O.K., O.K.—that's enough.

In the B.G. Pop can be seen approaching Nolan, Moose, Tommy, and Luke with a windbreaker jacket over his arm.

JACKIE

(a little hurt)

What's the matter wit' you, success gone to ya head?

TERRY

I told you lay off.

JACKIE

(to Chick in a falsetto)

My, ain't we touchy this morning?

MEDIUM CLOSE MEN BEHIND TERRY AT PIER ENTRANCE DAY

Nolan, Moose, Tommy, Luke, and others are muttering about Joey. Pop comes up to them. The men quickly drop the subject of Joey.

NOLAN

Go home, Pop. The lads who get work today 'll be chippin' in gladly.

TOMMY

Sure, we'll take care of ya.

LUKE

That's the truth, Pop.

Others mutter expressions of bitter sympathy. "Tough about Joey," etc.

POP

Thanks, boys, but I'm gonna shape. Who do you think's gonna pay for the funeral—Johnny Friendly and the boss stevedore?

CLOSE SHOT TERRY

Reacting.

Sonny, a few feet away, also hears and we follow him back to Pop and group.

SONNY

Hey, watch that talk. What you say?

NOLAN

He was just tellin' me how proud he was to belong to a fine honest local run by such an outstandin' labor leader as Johnny Friendly.

SONNY

Don't get wise now, you.

NOLAN

Wise! If I was wise I wouldn't be no longshoreman for thirty years and poorer now than when I started.

Sonny looks at him threateningly. Nolan holds his ground and Sonny goes on.

POP

Here—I brought you Joey's windbreaker—Wear it, Kayo. Yours is more full of holes than the Pittsburgh infield.

CLOSE SHOT NOLAN

He is affected, but largely hiding his feelings.

GROUP SHOT POP, NOLAN, MOOSE, TOMMY

J.P. Morgan pops up right behind Pop.

J.P.

Condolences. How you fixed for cabbage this mornin'?

NOLAN

Oh me and my chum are just rolling in the stuff. We only work down here for a hobby, J.P.

Pop's cronies chuckle.

MOOSE

Haw, haw, haw—that's a good one.

J.P.

(undaunted, to Pop)

You'll be needing a few dollars for your extras, won't you, Pop? You're three weeks behind on the last twenty-five, but I'm willing to take a chance.

NOLAN

Some chance—at ten percent a week! And if he don't borrow, he don't work.

J.P.

(to Pop)

You'll work.

NOLAN

I ought to belt you one, J.P.

J.P.

(retreating slightly)

Raise a hand to me and. . . .

NOLAN

. . . and you'll tell Johnny Friendly.

J.P.

You'd be off the pier for good.

POP

(ashamed)

All right, slip me a bill—and may you rot in hell, J.P.

J.P.

When I'm dead 'n gone you'll know what a friend I was.

NOLAN

Drop dead now, why don't you, so we c'n test your theory?

Moose leads the laughter. J.P. looks at them sourly.

J.P.

Condolences.

J.P. goes off with his shoulders bent over and his head down, like some mournful bird, and Nolan walks behind him, mimicking. Nolan notices Pop isn't laughing and stops.

CAMERA FOLLOWS J.P. toward Terry, Chick, and Jackie and holds on them. Two men in business suits, one of them carrying a briefcase, look decidedly out of place on the waterfront approach.

GLOVER

(larger, more good-natured of the two)

Do any of you men know Terry Malloy?

JACKIE

Malloy? Never head of 'im.

CHICK

(quickly)

Me neither.

They both turn away sullenly. Glover and his colleague, GILLETTE, look at Terry carefully. Gillette is scrappy and tough.

GLOVER

You're Terry Malloy, aren't you?

TERRY

(suspiciously)

What about it?

GLOVER

I thought I recognized you. Saw you fight in St. Nick's a couple of years ago.

TERRY

(impatiently)

O.K. O.K. Without the bird seed. What do you want?

GLOVER

Our identification.

He snaps out his wallet and holds it open for Terry's inspection.

TERRY

Waterfront—Crime—Commission—?

(pushes wallet back indignantly)

What's that?

GLOVER

We're getting ready to hold public hearings on waterfront crime and underworld infiltration of longshore unions.

TERRY

(automatically)

I don't know nothing.

GILLETTE

You haven't heard the questions yet.

GLOVER

(pleasantly)

There's a rumor that you're one of the last people to see Joey Doyle alive.

TERRY

And I still say—I don't know nothing.

GILLETTE

We're not accusing you of anything, Mr. Malloy.

GLOVER

I hope you understand that.

GILLETTE

We only want to ask you a few things about people you may know.

TERRY

People I—You mean sing for you. Get out of here before I—

GILLETTE

(with a slight but confident smile)

I wouldn't advise that, Mr. Malloy. Unless you want to be booked for assaulting an officer of the law.

TERRY

Listen, I don't know nothing, I didn't see nothing, I ain't saying nothing. So why don't you and your girl friend get lost.

GLOVER

(gently)

All right, Mr. Malloy, you have a right not to talk, if that's what you choose to do. But the public has a right to know the facts too.

GILLETTE

(nodding in agreement)

We may be seeing you again.

TERRY

Never will be much too soon.

GLOVER

(almost like a friend)

Take it easy.

The two men nod and turn away. Jackie and Chick, a few paces off, have been taking it in. Terry swaggers for their benefit.

TERRY

How do you like them jokers? Taking me for a pigeon.

JACKIE

(mimicking the investigators, in a falsetto)

Gimme the names. I'll write 'em down in me little book.

Chick laughs and punches Terry's arm with rough affection.

TERRY

(responding to the praise)

One more word 'n I would've belted the two of 'em, badge or no badge!

They nod and laugh approvingly.

There is a blast from the ship in the B.G. which is just docking.

MEDIUM CLOSE ON BIG MAC

The hiring boss. A stevedore official comes up to him with a box of slips.

STEVEDORE

Here's the tabs for two hundred banana carriers.

Big Mac blows his whistle.

MEDIUM CLOSE POP, NOLAN, ETC. PIER DAY

NOLAN

(trying to cheer Pop up)

A banana boat. It would be bananas. One of these days me ship's comin' in from Ireland, God love 'er, loaded to the gunnels with sweet Irish whiskey!

POP

Nolan, me lad, ye're dreamin' again.

They laugh, then Pop looks O.S. and frowns.

Edie?

LONG SHOT EDIE PIER DAY

From Pop's POV. Talking to a pier guard.

CLOSE ON POP

Standing with Kayo. About to start forward when the shape-up whistle blows, restraining him.

POP

(to Kayo)
What the devil is she doin' down here?

CLOSE ON EDIE AND PIER GUARD PIER DAY

GUARD

(with a brogue)
Edie, I know your father well, and I'm sorry for your troubles. But there's been hundreds of murders down here and practically no convictions—hardly any arrests.

EDIE

Why, Mr. Rourke? Why?

GUARD

The last fellow who talked was awful dead when they pulled him out of the river. I guess the Sisters don't teach you things like that up at your school in Tarrytown.
(with a gesture of futility)
That's the waterfront.

He shrugs his helplessness and turns away. Edie stands crestfallen. Then she turns in the opposite direction away from the pier.

EXT MEDIUM SHOT FATHER BARRY OUTSIDE PIER DAY
Father Barry is approaching.

EDIE

(surprised)
Father Barry.

FATHER BARRY

Hello, Edie.

EDIE

I'm afraid I spoke out of turn last night.

FATHER BARRY

You think I'm just a gravy-train rider in a turned-around collar?

She says nothing.
Don't you?

FATHER BARRY

(with humor)

I see the Sisters taught you not to lie.

She smiles in spite of herself.

FATHER BARRY

I been thinking about your question and the answer come up and hit me—bang. This is my parish. I don't know how much I can do but you're right, Edie—I'll never find out if I don't come down here and take a good look for myself.

She looks at him hopefully. O.S. a whistle blows again, shrilly. They turn in its direction.

MEDIUM CLOSE BIG MAC AT PIER ENTRANCE DAY

Putting his whistle away.

GROUP SHOT LONGSHOREMEN PIER DAY

Waiting silently, hopefully.

BIG MAC

The following men report to the loft—

CLOSER SHOT FAVORING TERRY

BIG MAC

Malloy.

Terry steps forward.

Hendricks, Krajowski. Now two hundred banana carriers.

He approaches the men.

CLOSE ON FATHER BARRY AND EDIE

Watching from the slip.

EDIE

Pop never talks about this.

Father Barry watches interestedly.

GROUP SHOT SHAPE-UP DAY

The men press closer to Big Mac, each one trying to attract his attention.

BIG MAC

Don't crowd me. Stand back.

AN OLD MAN

(seedy, toothless)

Give me a break, Mac. I been two weeks out of work.

MOOSE

I got five kids. I need a day bad.

A BEEFY LONGSHOREMAN

(old-fashioned looking in his knit stocking cap and heavy wool sweater)

How about me, Mac? I knew your old man.

BIG MAC

(roughly)

Come on, you bums, push back. I'll do the pickin'.

CLOSE SHOTS LONGSHOREMEN
From Big Mac's angle.

One touches an ear—another strokes his chin—another begs with his eyes—hungry, pleading, desperate faces.

CLOSE ON BIG MAC
Angrily trying to clear the way.

THE OLD MAN

I'll give four bucks for the job.

BEEFY LONGSHOREMAN

I'll kick in five.

BIG MAC

(shoving them hard)

Back! Get back!

The beefy longshoreman actually makes a grab for one of the tabs. The men begin to surround and engulf Mac. He is jostled and pushed. The beefy longshoreman, slightly behind Mac, suddenly knocks the box of tabs out of his hand.

BIG MAC

(desperately—over his shoulder)

Hey, Sonny! Truck!

FULL SHOT LONGSHOREMEN MELEE
Two hundred and fifty men scrambling on the ground, fighting for the tabs like animals.

CLOSE ON FATHER BARRY AND EDIE
Horrified, as they watch the struggle.

A SERIES OF SHOTS DETAILING BATTLE

CLOSE SHOT KAYO NOLAN
As he begins to rise, tab in hand, a big longshoreman at least a head taller swings a vicious punch at him. Kayo, with old-time boxing skill, "slips" it by a fraction of an inch. The effect could be a moment of comedy relief.

CLOSE SHOT MOOSE
On the ground—as he is about to pick up a tab, a heavy shoe steps on his hand and the tab is grabbed away from him.

CLOSE ON FATHER BARRY AND EDIE
Watching helplessly.

EDIE

Pop!

FREE-FOR-ALL FAVORING POP & TERRY
Pop is battling near the edge of the free-for-all, in view of Edie and Father Barry. He sees a tab on the ground and is about to pick it up when another man only slightly younger and bigger punches him in the nose. He retaliates with a looping punch that knocks his adversary back; but he is unable to scoop up the tab because meanwhile a crony of Terry's has called over.

JACKIE

Hey, Terry. Grab me one!

Terry reaches for it with one hand while blocking Pop off with his leg. He calls over to a crony.

TERRY

Here you go, Jackie boy.

As he hands it over to his chum, Pop comes charging in at Terry.

POP

Hey, give me that.

He swings wild punches at Terry. Just then Luke, the burly Negro

longshoreman, sees a tab behind Pop, hurls himself toward it, carrying Pop with him, and back into the battle royal.

EDIE
She has seen the above action and makes a beeline for Terry. She is furious!

EDIE
Give me that. It belongs to Pop. He saw it first.

Terry is enjoying himself. Unconsciously Edie is pressing herself against him to get the tab and her rage is a kind of passion that pleases him.

TERRY
Oh, I thought you was gonna go to work—with all them muscles.
(winks at Jackie, who laughs)

EDIE
Give it to me—my Pop's job—

TERRY

What makes him so special?

EDIE

None of your business.

TERRY

(to Jackie; handing him the tab)

Things're lookin' up on the docks, huh, Jackie?

JACKIE

Didn't you recognize him, dopey. That's Old Man *Doyle.*

TERRY

(losing his bravado)

Doyle.

(looks around at Pop, the identity hitting him)

Joey Doyle's. . . ?

(stares at Edie)

. . . You're his. . . .

EDIE

(firmly)

Sister. Yes I am.

He runs his hand over his face and then, with a sudden impulse:

TERRY

You don't want to lug bananas in the rain anyway, do you, Jackie?

He reaches over and takes the tab back from Jackie.

JACKIE

Aah, give it to 'im.

Terry hands the slip to Edie and adds, for the benefit of his pals:

TERRY

Here you go, muscles. Nice wrastlin' with you.

He flexes his forearm and throws two quick jabs at an imaginary opponent, a characteristic gesture. He sets his cap at a jaunty angle and winks at his chums but we feel his manner is forced, barely hiding his guilt. Edie looks after him with smoldering anger.

She turns as Father Barry comes into view, leading Pop. Pop's nose is bleeding and he is pretty thoroughly battered. Nolan joins him.

FATHER BARRY

Pop, you all right?

POP

(brusquely)

Sure, just the beak—

(taps his nose)

It's been busted before.

Edie hands him the tab.

EDIE

Here—I got it for you.

Pop takes it, but he is humiliated, and bitter that she should see him in this moment of weakness.

POP

Okay, I can use it—

(glares at her)

Now go back to the Sisters where you belong.

(His anger mounting with his need to regain his self-respect, he turns on Father Barry.)

I'm surprised with you, Father, if you don't mind my sayin' so. Lettin' her see things ain't fit for the eyes of a decent girl.

Just then Big Mac shouts from the pier opening.

BIG MAC

Hey, Doyle, you got a tab?

POP

(holding it up angrily)

Yeah!

BIG MAC

Then get in there. Number three gang, number one hatch, puh-ronto.

Pop jumps and hurries.

NOLAN

(following Pop)

Our welfare officer. He's been away three times for assault and battery.

MEDIUM CLOSE EDIE AND FATHER BARRY
Watching him go. Around them are at least one hundred rejected men who linger in resentful silence. Some of them are rubbing hands bruised in the melee. A truck, hurrying into the pier, sounds its horn loudly. The men barely avoid being run down.

BIG MAC
(angrily, to the rejected group)
Outa the way. Come back tomorra.

Father Barry looks at all this in amazement.

FATHER BARRY
(to one rejected man)
What do you do now?

The man shrugs, too beaten down to answer. Father Barry asks Luke:

What are you gonna do?

LUKE
(bitterly)
Like he says. Come back tomorra.

Luke goes along with Father Barry, who approaches Moose and Tommy, who have also been rejected.

FATHER BARRY
Is this what you do, just take it like this?

MOOSE
(carefully looking around and lowering his voice matter-of-factly)
Five straight mornin's I been standin' here and the bum looks right through me. There's always a couple hundred left standin' in the street.

TOMMY
(undertone)
Shh. Sonny's over there.

FATHER BARRY
And there's nothing you can do? How about your union?

MOOSE
(in an undertone)
You know how a blackjack local works, Father. Get up in a meetin', make a motion, the lights go out, you go out.

TOMMY

If three guys talk on a corner, Johnny's—
(He takes a careful look around.)
—boys break us up. Look at 'em.

FATHER BARRY

Didn't the miners—sailors—garment workers—get rid of this years ago?

TOMMY

The waterfront's tougher—like it ain't part of America. Anywhere else you got the law protectin' ya. Here ya just get knocked off and forgotten. Like—
(He stops.)

LUKE

(frightened)
Shh, not here, across the street.

MOOSE

River Street, you might as well be in—

Sonny and Truck move in.

SONNY

What is this, a church picnic? Get outa here. Excuse me, Father.

They all start away from the pier.

MOOSE

(looking to see if he is out of earshot)
That's how it's been ever since Johnny and his cowboys took over the local.

TOMMY

Name one place where it's even safe to talk.

FATHER BARRY

(impulsively)
Use the church.

LUKE

What?

FATHER BARRY

(after a significant pause)
The bottom of the church.

Father Barry has spoken in a normal voice, as contrasted with the whispering of the others, and they all look off toward Sonny and Truck to see if they have heard.

CLOSE ON SONNY
Watching them suspiciously.

BACK TO FATHER BARRY, EDIE AND GROUP

MOOSE
(still in an undertone)
You know what you're letting yourself in for, Father?

FATHER BARRY
Got a cigarette on you?
(As he is given one, he looks off.)

MEDIUM SHOT SONNY
From Father Barry's angle.

MEDIUM CLOSE FATHER BARRY

FATHER BARRY
(his voice decisive)
You heard me, boys. Use the bottom of the church.

Father Barry looks at Edie.

DISSOLVE

INT MEDIUM SHOT PIER LOFT DAY
In this long area atop the working pier various articles of cargo are stored. Elderly men work at a leisurely pace.

CLOSE SHOT PILE OF COFFEE BAGS DAY
On top of which Terry is lying comfortably reading a comic book. Charley enters to him.

CHARLEY
Working hard?

TERRY
It's a living.

He wriggles himself deeper into the coffee bags.

CHARLEY
(looking up at him)
You don't mind working once in a while to justify this lofty position?

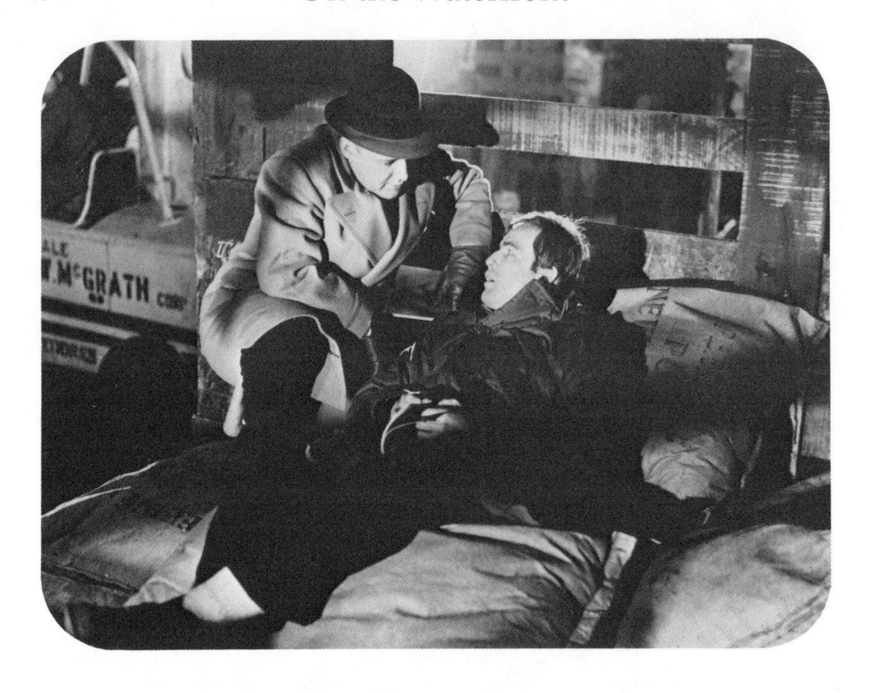

TERRY

I just finished work. I counted the bags.

CHARLEY

We got a little extra detail for you. The local priest and this Doyle girl are getting up a meeting in the church. We'd like a run-down on it. You know, names and numbers of all the players. You're nominated.

TERRY

(frowns)

Why me, Charley? I'd feel funny going in there.

CHARLEY

(indicating this job)

Johnny does you favors, kid. You got to do a little one for him once in a while.

TERRY

But going in that church, I'd be stooling for you, Charley. You make a pigeon out of me.

CHARLEY

(tolerantly)

Let me explain you something, kid. Stooling is when you rat on your friends, on the guys you're with.

(sees Terry frown)

When Johnny needs a favor, don't try to figure it out, just do it. Now go ahead, join the congregation.

DISSOLVE

INT ENTRANCEWAY TO LOWER LEVEL CHURCH EVENING

This is an overflow chapel for the church above. There are stained glass windows, an altar, pews and the figures of saints, but all is utter simplicity; it has not lost its basement feeling, and the unadorned walls and low lighting may suggest the catacombs.

The above is seen from the POV of Terry as he approaches. Inside Father Barry faces a small group of longshoremen still in their work clothes, including Nolan, Moose, Tommy, and Luke; Edie sits behind them. A thin-faced, rather ascetic-looking priest, FATHER VINCENT, sits disapprovingly in the rear. As Terry stands in the rear, not anxious to enter, Father Barry is saying:

FATHER BARRY

(rapidly, with a cigarette in his mouth)

I thought there'd be more of you here, but—the Romans found out what a handful could do, if it's the right handful. And the same goes for you and the mob that's got their foot on your neck. I'm just a potato-eater but isn't it simple as one-two-three? One—The working conditions are bad. Two—They're bad because the mob does the hiring. Three—The only way to break the mob is to stop letting them get away with murder.

He looks around at them. Everybody is silent, waiting.

If just one of you would answer one question, we'd have a start.

(pause)

And that question is—Who killed Joey Doyle?

REVERSE ON GROUP

Silence. Moose looks down at the floor. Nolan works his left fist into the palm of his right hand. Tommy runs his hand over his face, embarrassed. Luke stares straight ahead of him. Terry sets his jaw stubbornly. Edie looks at all of them with a hopeful, pleading intensity.

Father Barry waits, and then asks again—

FATHER BARRY

Not one of you has a line on—who killed Joey Doyle?

Silence.

I've got a hunch every one of you could tell us something about it.

Silence.

Then answer this one—How can we call ourselves Christians and protect these murderers with our silence?

Silence. The Father looks from one to the other, hoping for some break in the ranks.

Terry starts down the aisle, just as Edie turns on Tommy.

EDIE

Tommy Collins, you were Joey's best friend. How can you just sit there and not be saying anything?

TOMMY

(miserably)

I'll always think of him as my best friend, but—

He falls silent and shakes his head. Next to him, Nolan notices Terry.

NOLAN

(muttering to Moose)

Who asked him here?

FATHER BARRY

(to Terry)

Have a seat. I'm trying to find out just what happened to Joey Doyle. Maybe you can help.

Terry is tight-lipped.

NOLAN

(whispering loudly to Moose)

The brother of Charley the Gent. They'll help us get to the bottom of the river.

TERRY

(turns around angrily)

Keep Charley out of this.

NOLAN

(spunkily)

You don't think he'd be—helpful?

TERRY

(insolently)

Go ask him, why don't you? Ask himself yourself.

NOLAN

Maybe I will—one of these days.

TERRY

(laughs scornfully)

One of these days.

They glare at each other. Edie regards Terry with curiosity.

FATHER BARRY

(cutting through)

Now listen, if you know who the pistols are, if you see them on the dock every day, are you going to keep still until they cut you down one by one?

(turns from one to the other)

Are you? Are you? How about you, Nolan?

NOLAN

Father, one thing you got to understand. On the dock we've always been D 'n D.

FATHER BARRY

(puzzled)

D 'n D?

NOLAN

(nodding)

Deef 'n dumb. Somethin' c'n happen right in front of our noses and we don't see nothin'. You know what I mean. No matter how much we hate the torpedoes we don't rat.

Moose, Luke, and others mutter agreement.

FATHER BARRY

Boys, get smart. I know you're gettin' pushed around but one thing we got in this country is ways of fightin' back. Gettin' the facts to the public. Testifyin' for what you know is right against what you know is wrong. What's ratting to them is telling the truth for you. Can't you see that?

(turns from one to another)

Huh? Huh?

The men do not respond. A few look back at Terry apprehensively. Father Barry subsides, feeling defeated. Father Vincent comes forward and takes over the meeting.

FATHER VINCENT

(dismissing them)

This seems to be just about all we can do at this time, I think you'll agree, Father, and so I'd like to close with a few words from St. Paul, "Come unto me. . . ."

He is interrupted by the shattering of glass as a rock comes hurtling through the long narrow stained-glass window. Everyone looks at each other in alarm. Some jump up.

NOLAN

(thumbing toward the window)

That's our friends.

CLOSE UP TERRY

Looking at Edie; then he cases the room for other exits.

MEDIUM CLOSE FATHER BARRY AND FATHER VINCENT

FATHER VINCENT

What did I tell you about sticking your neck out?

FATHER BARRY

These fellers need help, Vince.

FATHER VINCENT

(striding off)

Okay. Don't blame me when they pack you off to Abyssinia.

FATHER BARRY

I'll take my chances.

(turns toward the group, picking up the rock)

We must be on the right track or they wouldn't be sending us this little calling card.

FATHER BARRY

(continued)

(pause)

Who's got a cigarette?

(as he takes one)

You better go home in pairs.

They all start out tensely, Father Barry helping to pair them off at the door. Edie lingers behind them, frightened. As she starts forward, Terry suddenly approaches.

TERRY

Not that way.

She looks at him in surprise. Terry pulls her back with rough solicitousness.

Come on, I'll get you out.

Before she has time to protest he is leading her rapidly to another exit.

DISSOLVE

EXT LONG SHOT CHURCH EXIT DAY

Moose and Nolan come down the steps of the church. They do not realize they are being ambushed but the audience does. The goons leap out at them, and we see the effect of this action in the giant shadows across the face of the church, the flailing bats looming as large as telephone poles. We hear the cries of pain, then groans.

EXT MEDIUM CLOSE STREET DUSK

As Father Barry runs up, Sonny and Truck are working Nolan over with baseball bats. Father Barry wrestles with them, taking a glancing blow in consequence, and the goons take off. Nolan sinks to the sidewalk with blood streaming from his head and Father Barry kneels beside him.

FATHER BARRY

You all right, Nolan?

NOLAN

(furiously)

Yeah, considerin' they was usin' my head for a baseball!

FATHER BARRY

(taking a handkerchief to blot the blood on Nolan's face)

Nice fellows.

NOLAN

(rubbing his head angrily)

Those blood suckers. How I'd love to fix those babies but—

FATHER BARRY

But you still hold out for silence?

Nolan hesitates.

You still call it ratting?

NOLAN

Are you on the level, Father?

FATHER BARRY

What do you think?

NOLAN

If I stick my neck out, and they chopped it off, would that be the end of it? Or are you ready to go all the way?

FATHER BARRY

I'll go down the line, Kayo, believe me.

NOLAN

Baseball bats—that's just for openers. They'll put the muscle on you, turned-around collar or no turned-around collar.

FATHER BARRY

And I still say you stand up and I'll stand up with you.

NOLAN

Down to the wire?

FATHER BARRY

So help me God!

NOLAN

Well, I had my fun, I've drunk my fill and I tickled some good-lookin' fillies—I'm on borried time.

Nolan says this with a slight smile as he makes an effort to rise.

FATHER BARRY

(as he helps Nolan to his feet with a grin)

We're off and running, Kayo.

MEDIUM CLOSE AT CHURCH ENTRANCE DUSK

Father Vincent is nervously closing the doors.

EXT RECTORY FIRE ESCAPE DAY

Leading down to a dark side street. Terry pulls Edie along at a flying pace. He jumps down from the bottom landing, then looks up to catch her, for whom the height is too great. He holds her for a moment. Then he stops and listens. Heavy rapid footsteps approach. It is Moose and Luke, closely followed by goons wielding baseball bats. Terry pulls Edie back against the wall into the shadows. The goons run past and Terry starts racing with Edie down a narrow alley in the opposite direction.

MEDIUM CLOSE WATERFRONT STREET NIGHT

The one that meets the alley at the other end. As Terry reaches the street with Edie, he looks around to be sure all's quiet.

TERRY

(looking back)

I think we're O.K.

EDIE

(catching her breath)

Thanks.

(shakes her head)

Steel pipes and baseball bats.

TERRY

They play pretty rough.

EDIE

(puzzled)

Which side are you with?

TERRY

(pointing to himself)

I'm with Terry.

EDIE

(straightening her dress)

I'll get home all right now.

TERRY

I better see you get there.

She looks at him wonderingly. The rummy longshoreman, Mutt Murphy, shuffles over toward Edie with his hand out, frightening her closer to Terry.

MUTT

A dime. One thin dime for a cup of coffee.

TERRY

Coffee, that's a laugh. His belly is used to nothing but rotgut whiskey.

MUTT

(ignoring Terry and coming closer to Edie)

One little dime you don't need?

(He brings his whiskered, sodden face very close to Edie's and stares at her as if through a dense fog.)

I know you—you're Edie Doyle. Your brother's a saint—

(crosses himself quickly)

—only one ever tried to get me my compensation.

He points a wavering (unconsciously accusing) finger at Terry.

Remember, Terry, you was there the night he was. . . ?

CLOSE UP EDIE STREET NIGHT

Looking at Terry in surprise.

TERRY

(nervously reaching into his pocket)

Yeah, yeah—here's half a buck, go have yourself a ball.

MUTT

I can't believe it—a small fortune.

(He kisses the coin, then pulls from his shirt a small tobacco pouchful of coins in which he deposits this one.)

(then turns on Terry again)

You can't buy me—you're still a bum!

(raises his cap to Edie with unexpected formality)

'Bye, Edie. Lord have mercy on Joey.

(crosses himself quickly and he goes off)

TERRY

(sourly)

Look who says *bum!*

EDIE

(looking after Mutt)

Everybody loved Joey. From the little kids to the old rummies.

(looks up at Terry)

Did you know him very well?

TERRY

(evasively)

Everybody knew him. He got around.

EDIE

(looking after Mutt)

What did that man mean when he said you were. . . ?

TERRY

(quickly)

Aah, he's a bottlebaby, he talks to himself, the joke of the neighborhood.

EDIE

(glancing at him and then hurrying her steps)

I better get home.

She gives Terry as wide a berth as possible.

TERRY

Don't be afraid of me. I ain't going to bite you.

She continues to walk apart from him.

What's the matter, they don't let you walk with fellers where you've been?

EDIE

You know how the Sisters are.

TERRY

You training to be a nun or something?

EDIE

(smiles)

It's a regular college. It's just run by the nuns. The Sisters of St. Anne.

TERRY

And you spend all your time just learning stuff, huh?

EDIE

(smiling at the way he puts it)

I want to be a teacher.

TERRY

A teacher! Dong!!!

(He's impressed.)

You know I admire brains. Take my brother Charley. He's very brainy. Very.

EDIE

(quietly)

It isn't brains. It's how you use them.

TERRY

(increasingly impressed, almost awe-struck)

Yeah. Yeah. I get your thought. You know I seen you lots of times before. Parochial school on Pulaski Street? Seven, eight years ago? Your hair come down in—

EDIE

In braids? That's right.

TERRY

Looked like two pieces of rope. And your teeth were—

EDIE

(smiling)

I know. I thought I'd never get those braces off.

TERRY

(laughs)

Man, you were a mess!

EDIE

I can get home all right from here—

TERRY

The thought I'm tryin' to get over is you grew up beauteeful. Remember me?

EDIE

(nodding)

The moment I saw you.

TERRY

(strutting)

Some people got faces that stick in your mind.

EDIE

(tenderly)

I remember you were in trouble all the time.

TERRY

Now you got me! It's a wonder I wasn't punchy by the time I was twelve. The rulers those Sisters used to whack me with!

(cracks himself on the head and laughs)

They thought they could beat an education into me—I foxed 'em.

EDIE

Maybe they just didn't know how to handle you.

TERRY

(warming to the subject)

How would you've done it?

EDIE

With a little more patience and kindness. That's what makes people mean and difficult. Nobody cares enough about them.

Terry plays "Hearts and Flowers" on an imaginary violin. Edie watches curiously.

What's that?

TERRY

Pardon me while I reach for my beads.

EDIE

What?

TERRY

What-what? Where you been the last four five years? Outer space?

EDIE

When Mother died Pop sent me out to school in the country. He was afraid with no one home I'd—get into bad company.

TERRY

(righteously)

Well he played it smart. Too many good-for-nothin's around here. All they got on their mind's a little beer, a little pool, a little—

TERRY

(continued)

(looks at her and catches himself, his face registering: I'm with a Nice—Girl)

I better get you home.

DISSOLVE

EXT TENEMENT SUNDAY AFTERNOON

Overhead a flock of pigeons sweep by, close enough for the flapping of their wings to be heard.

Terry and Edie approach the stoop.

TERRY

(looking up)

Boy, they sure fly nice, don't they?

EDIE

(surprised)

Do you like pigeons?

TERRY

That's my own flock up there, getting their evening workout. I won plenty of races with 'em.

(impulsively)

Listen, you want to see them? Come up on the roof with me and I'll show 'em to you.

They have reached the stoop of Edie's tenement.

EDIE

I'd better go in.

TERRY

(not wanting to let go of her)

I only live up there and across the roof.

EDIE

(going in)

Thanks anyway.

TERRY

(following her)

Listen, Edie, am I going to see you again?

EDIE

(simply)

What for?

TERRY

(suddenly bewildered)

I don't know.

EDIE

I really don't know.

Then she goes in abruptly. Terry is left standing there, staring after her, confused by the unfamiliar emotion he is feeling for her. Suddenly his thoughts are interrupted by—

MEDIUM CLOSE MRS. COLLINS

The sound of a lower-floor window opening as Mrs. Collins sticks her head out.

MRS. COLLINS

You got some nerve.

TERRY

What do you mean?

CLOSE SHOT EDIE
Overhearing, as she enters the house.

MEDIUM CLOSE TERRY AND MRS. COLLINS

MRS. COLLINS
You know what I mean. Leave her alone.

TERRY
(apologetically)
I was only talkin' to her.

MRS. COLLINS
She's off limits for bums like you. Leave her alone.

TERRY
I can look at her, can't I? It's a free country.

MRS. COLLINS
(as she goes)
Not *that* free.
She closes window.

EDIE INTERIOR ON STAIRS
She mounts the stairs, thinking about what she has just heard. We are close on her face, as she approaches the door to their place.

INT EDIE'S BEDROOM EVENING
As Edie enters, Pop, in his undershirt, favorite attire, is just putting the last articles into Edie's suitcase. He snaps the suitcase shut. There is an old cat on the bed.

POP
You're all packed.
(reaches into his pocket)
And here's your bus ticket. You're on your way back to St. Anne's.

EDIE
Pop, I'm not ready to go back yet.

POP
Edie, for years we pushed quarters into a cookie jar, to keep you up there with the Sisters, and to keep you from things like I just seen out the window. My own daughter arm-in-arm with Terry Malloy. You know who Terry Malloy is?

EDIE

(simply)
Who is he, Pop?

POP

(mimics)
Who is he! Edie, you're so soft-hearted and soft-headed you wouldn't recognize the devil if he had you by the throat. You know who this Terry Malloy is? The kid brother of Charlie the Gent, Johnny Friendly's right hand, a butcher in a camel hair coat.

EDIE

Are you trying to tell me Terry is too?

POP

(shouting)
I'm not trying to tell you he's Little Lord Fauntleroy.

EDIE

He tries to act tough, but there's a look in his eyes that. . . .

POP

A look in his eyes! Hold your hats, brother, here we go again. You think he's one of those cases you're always draggin' in and feelin' sorry for. Like the litter of kittens you had—the only one she wants to keep has six toes and it's cockeyed to boot. Look at him. The bum! And the crush you had on that little Abyssinian. . . .

EDIE

He wasn't Abyssinian, Pop, Assyrian. . . .

POP

Six-toed cats. Assyrians. Abyssinians. It's the same difference. Well don't think this Terry Malloy is any six-toed cockeyed Assyrian. He's a bum. Charley and Johnny Friendly owned him when he was a fighter and when they ring the bell he still goes into action.

EDIE

(musing)
He wanted to see me again.

POP

You think we kept you out in Tarrytown just to have you go walkin' with a corner saloon hoodlum like Terry Malloy? Now get back to Tarrytown, before I put a strap to you.

EDIE

(flaring)

And learn about charity and justice and all the other things people would rather talk about than practice?

Pop goes up to her and holds out his two arms, his right one closer to Edie; he trembles with emotion.

POP

See this arm? It's two inches longer'n the other one. That's years of workin' and sweatin', liftin' and swingin' a hook. And every time I heisted a box or a coffee bag I says to myself—this is for Edie, so she can be a teacher or somethin' decent. I promised your mother. You better not let her down.

Suddenly touched, Edie goes up to Pop and kisses him.

EDIE

Pop, don't think I'm not feeling grateful for all you've done to get me an education and shelter me from this.

(becoming aroused)

But now my eyes are open. I see things I know are so wrong how can I go back and keep my mind on things that are only in books and that people aren't living? I'm staying, Pop. And I'm going to keep on trying to find out who's guilty for Joey. I'd walk home with a dozen Terry Malloys if I thought they could help me. I tell you I'm staying, Pop.

Pop starts to pull his belt out of his trousers.

POP

You are like—

EDIE

(with regret and affection)

Pop!

She turns and runs out. Pop with his belt in one hand, takes a few steps after her and then stops and stares at the unused bus ticket.

POP

(shaking his head as he mutters)

Jesus, Mary and Joseph—I was cursed with stubborn children—keep an eye on her.

EXT TENEMENT ROOFTOP EVENING

Autumn on the roof. It is not particularly romantic—there are clotheslines, wooden boxes, etc. But to the people of this neighborhood it is a luxurious terrace. Terry's birds are aloft, flying in a great circle, nicely silhouetted against the sun-drenched evening sky. Jimmy Conners is with him. Terry has a long pole with which he keeps the birds circling. Moose is leaning against the wall, playing an Irish melody on his harmonica. His wife, a heavyset woman, sits beside him.

MOOSE'S WIFE

(moving her feet)

My feet feels like dancin'. But the rest of me just feels like settin' here.

MEDIUM SHOT TERRY

As he swings his pole he looks off and sees—

LONG SHOT EDIE ROOFTOP EVENING

Hurrying toward him across the rooftops.

MEDIUM CLOSE TERRY ROOFTOP EVENING

Catching sight of her, and stopping to admire her as she comes toward him.

TERRY

(to Jimmy)

Okay—I guess they got enough exercise. Let 'em come in.

He puts down the pole and the birds start flying down toward the coop. He sees Edie approach.

JIMMY

I wonder how long she's goin' to hang around, huh, Terry?

TERRY

(indicating the pigeons)

Be sure they got enough water.

And he turns to await Edie.

SHOT BRINGING EDIE TO TERRY

EDIE

I changed my mind. I feel real mean tonight.

TERRY

(pleased)

Good. So do I.

As Jimmy goes off to fetch some water, Edie reads the fancy lettering on the back of his jacket.

EDIE

The Golden Warriors.

TERRY

I started them Golden Warriors. I was their first Supreme Commander.

Now Jimmy starts back toward them.

My shadow. He follows me around like I was Mickey Mantle. Thinks I'm a big man because I boxed pro for a while.

(throws a few quick jabs)

Several pigeons swoop down and enter the coop. He nods towards her.

Here they come! The champion flock of the neighborhood.

EDIE

You don't mind yourself at all, do you.

(turns to the birds)

Joey used to race pigeons.

TERRY

(darkening)

He had a few birds.

(pauses, nods toward Joey's coop across the roof)

I got up and fed 'em this morning.

EDIE

That was nice of you.

TERRY

(disconcerted, needing to talk)

I like pigeons. You send a bird five hundred miles away he won't stop for food or water until he's back in his own coop.

EDIE

I wouldn't have thought you'd be so interested—in pigeons.

TERRY

I go for this stuff. You know this city's full of hawks? There must be twenty thousand of 'em. They perch on top of the big hotels and swoop down on the pigeons in the park.

EDIE

(slightly horrified)

The things that go on.

TERRY

(proudly indicating a large pigeon in the coop)

How do you like that one?

EDIE

Oh she's a beauty.

JIMMY

(critically)

She's a he. His name is Swifty.

TERRY
My lead bird. He's always on that top perch.

EDIE
He looks awful proud of himself.

JIMMY
Why shouldn't he—he's the boss.

TERRY
If another fella tries to take that perch away from him, he lets him have it.

EDIE
Even pigeons aren't peaceful.

TERRY
One thing about them though, they're faithful. They get married just like people.

JIMMY
Better.

TERRY
Yeah, once they're mated they stay together all their lives until one of 'em dies.

EDIE
That's nice.

They look at each other, both strangely upset.

TERRY
(suddenly)
Listen, you like beer?

EDIE
I don't know.

TERRY
Want to go out and have one with me?

EDIE
In a saloon?

TERRY
(imploring)
Come on, I know a quiet one, with a special entrance for ladies. . . .

DISSOLVE

INT SALOON LADIES' SIDE NIGHT

Perhaps a sign can emphasize *Ladies' Entrance*. As Terry leads Edie in, a tipsy Irish biddy is noisily protesting her enforced departure.

WOMAN

—I'm only after havin' one more wee bit—

BARTENDER

You and your *one-mores*. Now beat it.

As Terry and Edie reach the bar, the radio blares a baseball game. A roar goes up from the speaker. Bartender nods to Terry. In the corner a small well-oiled longshoreman sings "I'll Take You Home Again, Kathleen" in a plaintive, cracking voice.

BARTENDER

Well, what do you know—Jackie just stole home.

TERRY

(glancing at Edie with a mischievous wink at the bartender)

I wouldn't mind doing that myself.

The bartender grins. Terry guides Edie to a small table.

(to Edie)

What're you drinking?

Edie hesitates, obviously not knowing what to ask for. A customer at the bar says, loudly—

SINGER OF "KATHLEEN"

(B.G.)

Give me a Glockenheimer.

EDIE

(it could be root beer for all she knows)

I'll try a—Glockenheimer.

TERRY

(to bartender)

Likewise. And draw two for chasers.

(to Edie)

Now you're beginning to live.

EDIE

(as the drinks are poured)

I am?

Edie picks up her glass, sniffs the contents with some distaste and then sips it tentatively. Terry watches with amusement.

TERRY

(still swaggering)

Not that way—like this.

(holds glass up)

Down the hatch!

(gulps it down)

Wham!

Edie takes her drink and does likewise. She gasps and her eyes pop.

EDIE

(with soft amazement)

Wham. . . .

TERRY

(grinning at her)

How you like it?

EDIE

It's quite—
(gulps)
—nice.

TERRY

How about another one?

EDIE

(already feeling this one)
No thanks. . . .

TERRY

(to bartender)
Hit me again, Mac.

BARTENDER

(as he pours drink)
See the fight last night? That Riley—both hands. Little bit on your style.

TERRY

Hope he has better luck.

EDIE

Were you really a prizefighter?

TERRY

(nods)
I went pretty good for a while, didn't I, Al? But—I didn't stay in shape—and—
(a little ashamed)
—I had to take a few dives.

EDIE

A dive? You mean, into the water?

TERRY

(laughs harshly)
Naw, in the ring, a dive is—

He stops, shakes his head and with his finger draws an invisible square in the air.

EDIE

(mystified)
Now what are you doing?

TERRY

Describing you. A square from out there. I mean you're nowhere.

(draws it again)

Miss Four Corners.

EDIE

(smiles, but persistent)

What made you want to be a fighter?

TERRY

I had to scrap all my life. Figured I might as well get paid for it. When I was a kid my old man got killed—never mind how. Charley and I was put in a place—they called it a Children's Home. Some home! I run away and peddled papers, fought in club smokers and—

(catches himself)

But what am I runnin' off at the mouth for? What do you care?

EDIE

Shouldn't we care about everybody?

TERRY

What a fruitcake you are!

EDIE

Isn't everybody part of everybody else?

TERRY

Gee, thoughts! Alla time thoughts!

(then)

You really believe that drool?

EDIE

(deeply shocked)

Terry!

TERRY

Want to hear my philosophy? Do it to him before he does it to you.

EDIE

(aroused)

Our Lord said just the opposite.

TERRY

I'm not lookin' to get crucified. I'm lookin' to stay in one piece.

EDIE

(flaring up)

I never met such a person. Not a spark of romance or sentiment or—or human kindness in your whole body.

TERRY

What do they do for you, except get in your way?

EDIE

And when things get in your way—or people—you just knock them aside—get rid of them—is that your idea?

TERRY

(defensive—stung)

Listen—get this straight—don't look at me when you say them things. It wasn't my fault what happened to your brother. Fixing Joey wasn't my idea. . . .

EDIE

(gently)

Why, Terry, who said it was?

TERRY

(lamely)

Well, nobody, I guess. But that Father Barry, I didn't like the way he kept lookin' at me.

EDIE

He was looking at everybody the same way. Asking the same question.

TERRY

(troubled, not convinced)

Yeah, yeah. . . .

(suddenly)

This Father Barry, what's his racket?

EDIE

(shocked)

His—racket?

TERRY

(trying to regain his bravado)

You've been off in daisyland, honey. Everybody's got a racket.

EDIE

But a priest. . . ?

With his finger he again describes a square in the air and then points through it to Edie. This time it angers her.

EDIE

You don't believe anything, do you?

TERRY

Edie, down here it's every man for himself. It's keepin' alive! It's standin' in with the right people so you can keep a little loose change jinglin' in your pocket.

EDIE

And if you don't?

TERRY

If you don't. . . .

(points downward with a descending whistle)

Keep your neck in and your nose clean and you'll never have no trouble down here.

EDIE

But that's living like an animal—

Terry seems almost to illustrate this by the way he drains off his beer and wipes his mouth with his sleeve.

TERRY

I'd rather live like an animal than end up like—

He hesitates.

EDIE

Like Joey? Are you afraid to mention his name?

TERRY

(challenged—defensive)

Why keep harpin' on it?

(looks at her unfinished beer)

Come on, drink up. You got to get a little fun out of life. What's the matter with you?

(nods toward juke box)

I'll play you some music.

He starts toward the juke box. She turns with him. Suddenly something cries out in her, almost as if she didn't know she was going to say it—

EDIE

Help me, if you can—for God's sakes help me!

CLOSE ON TERRY

For the first time the edge is knocked off his swagger. He feels the purity of her grief. He'd like to help—that's his immediate reaction. But there's his brother Charley and his steady work and his loyalties to the mob and its code. All this runs through his mind, confusing him, tearing him. . . .

CLOSE ON TERRY AND EDIE

Terry turns back to her, with a helpless gesture.

TERRY

I—I'd like to, Edie, but—

(shakes his head)

—there's nothin' I can do.

Edie feels subdued, ashamed at breaking down. She rises, and in a low voice says—

EDIE

All right, all right . . . I shouldn't've asked you.

TERRY

You haven't finished your beer.

EDIE

I don't want it. But why don't you stay and finish your drink.

TERRY

(swinging off the stool)

I got my whole life to drink.

As if magnetized by her, he follows her out.

EXT LADIES' BAR NIGHT

As Terry comes up alongside her.

TERRY

You're not sore at me?

EDIE

(with complete innocence)

What for?

TERRY

For—not being any help?

She looks at him with disturbing simplicity.

EDIE

Why no—I think you would if you could. . . .

CLOSE UP TERRY

Struck. Her faith in him and in human nature becomes the most painful kind of accusation.

TWO-SHOT EDIE AND TERRY STREET NIGHT

Softly, silently, she begins to cry.

TERRY

(gently)

What are you crying for?

EDIE

(shaking her head)

I thought I felt mean tonight. But I'm not—I'm just—all mixed up. . . .

Ahead of them down the block is an outdoor neighborhood party. The rhythm of a small band reaches out to them.

Edie hangs back and Terry takes her hand.

TERRY

Come on, I'll walk you through. It's the shortest way home.

He takes her hand and she walks along with him passively. The street is illuminated with colored lights and bright paper streamers. There are several gaily decorated counters serving drinks and sandwiches. There are balloons and colored paper hats. Neighbors are dancing in the street. Children look on, a few mimicking their elders from the sidelines. Above the street is a homemade banner inscribed: JUST MARRIED—JOHNNY AND MARY O'DAY! We catch a glimpse of the happy young bridal couple, as Terry and Edie reach the edge of the celebrants. Her eyes light up. She has passed into a dreamlike forgetfulness.

TERRY

You like music?

Edie nods dreamily.

—and dancing?

Edie nods again.

TERRY

(pulling her to him before she realizes what has happened)

We're on!

At first Edie dances somewhat clumsily and stiffly but gradually begins to dance with zest and surprising skill, as if a whole suppressed side of her nature were suddenly being released. Terry is light on his feet and they do some intricate steps together.

Hey, we're good!

(grins at her)

The Sisters should see you now, huh?

She laughs, out of her youth and embarrassment and unexpected enjoyment of a stolen moment.

Now Terry draws her to him and they dance a more conventional half-time foxtrot to the music.

TERRY

(awkwardly)

I—I never knew a girl like you, Edie. I always knew the kind you just grab 'em and—I never knew a girl like you, Edie.

EDIE

It's fun dancing with your eyes closed. I'm floating. I'm floating. . . .

They have danced off to a darker, less populated section of the street, away from the bar and the bandstand. Behind them people are dancing and laughing. Terry's lips brush her cheek as they dance, and move on to her mouth.

TERRY

(breathlessly)

Edie. . . .

Carried away, she allows him to kiss her and even responds. Then Terry feels someone tapping him on the shoulder.

He wheels around to see—

CLOSE SHOT BARNEY STREET NIGHT
Barney wears a colored paper hat.

BARNEY

I been looking for you, Terry. The boss wants you.

THREE-SHOT TERRY, EDIE AND BARNEY STREET NIGHT
While the music and dancing continue around them.

TERRY

Right now?

BARNEY

(nods)

He just got a call from "Mr. Upstairs." Something's gone wrong. He's plenty hot.

TERRY

I'm gonna take her home first.

BARNEY

I'd get over there, Terry. I'll take the little lady home.

TERRY

(for Edie's benefit)

I'll come over when I'm ready.

BARNEY

You know Johnny when he gets mad.

As suddenly as Barney arrived, he ducks off.

CLOSE ON TERRY AND EDIE STREET NIGHT
Edie senses Terry's distraction.

EDIE

(puzzled)

Who was that?

She is about to move away; Terry puts his hand on her arm.

TERRY

(impulsively)

Edie, listen, stay out of this mess. Quit tryin' to ask things about Joey. It ain't safe for you.

EDIE

Why worry about me? You're the one who says only look out for yourself.

TERRY

(pent up with his guilt and his frustrated feeling for her)

Okay, get in hot water. But don't come hollerin' to me when you get burned.

EDIE

Why should I come hollering to you at all?

TERRY

Because . . . because. . . .

(apologetically, as if this were a sign of weakness)

Listen, Edie, don't get sore now—but I think we're getting in love with each other.

EDIE

(really fighting against it)

I can't let myself fall in love with you.

TERRY

(fervently)

That goes double for me.

As they stare at each other in entangled hostility and love, a man turns from the food counter behind them, just finishing a hot dog and steps into Terry's path. It is Mr. Glover, the Commission investigator. In the B.G. is Gillette.

GLOVER

Mr. Malloy, I was hoping I might find you here.

Terry turns as if to dart off. Glover puts a restraining hand on his arm.

You're being served with a subpoena, Mr. Malloy.

TERRY

What?

GLOVER

(reaching quickly into his briefcase)

Be at the State House, Courtroom Nine, at ten o'clock tomorrow.

TERRY

I told you I don't know nothin' and I ain't saying nothin'.

GLOVER

You can bring a lawyer if you wish. And you're privileged under the Constitution to protect yourself against questions that might implicate you in any crimes.

TERRY

(more in pain then anger now)

You know what you're askin'? You're askin'—

GILLETTE

(stepping in from B.G.)

(sternly)

Mr. Malloy, all we're asking you to do is tell the truth.

GLOVER

(more gently)

Goodnight, kid.

Terry looks at the subpoena in tortured confusion.

EDIE

(softly)

What are you going to do?

TERRY

(viciously—reverting to type)

I won't eat cheese for no cops, that's for sure.

EDIE

(with sudden intuition)

It was Johnny Friendly who killed Joey, wasn't it?

Terry looks off and then looks down, unable to speak.

He had him killed or had something to do with it, didn't he? He and your brother Charley?

Terry drops his eyes again; he can say nothing.

You can't tell me, can you? Because you're part of it. You're as bad as the worst of them, aren't you, Terry? Aren't you? Tell me the truth!

TERRY

Edie, your old man's right, go back to that school out in daisyland. You're driving yourself nuts—you're driving me nuts—stop worrying about the truth—worry about yourself.

EDIE

Look out for number one. Always number one.

(her voice rising in anger)

I should've known you wouldn't tell me. Pop said Johnny Friendly used to own you. I think he still owns you.

(then gently, and hating to have to say it)

No wonder everybody calls you a bum.

TERRY

(as if struck)

Don't say that, Edie, don't. . . .

Edie is crying softly, without sobs.

EDIE

(with a half-sob)

It's true.

TERRY

I'm tryin' to keep you from being hurt—What more do you want?

EDIE

Much more, Terry. Much, much more!

She runs off. Terry looks after her, pained; the subpoena weighs in his hand. He stares at it in agony, while the party swirls around him. Then the blare of an auto horn cuts through the music.

VOICE OF JOHNNY

(O.S.)

Hey, genius.

Terry looks up.

MEDIUM LONG SHOT

Johnny Friendly's black Cadillac parked across the street. A driver, Sonny, Truck, Big Mac, and Charley are in it. Terry hurries up to them.

TERRY

(lamely)

I—I was just on my way up, Johnny.

JOHNNY

By way of Chicago?

Sonny starts to laugh but Johnny cuts him short.

How many times you been knocked out, Terry?

TERRY

(surprised)

Only two times, why, Johnny?

(Throughout the following tirade, Charley would like to intervene in Terry's behalf, but Johnny roughly nudges him into silence.)

JOHNNY

It must have been once too often. I think your brains come apart. What you got up there, Chinese bells?

TERRY

Aw, Johnny. . . .

JOHNNY

I thought you were gonna keep an eye on that church meeting.

TERRY

Nothing happened, Johnny.

JOHNNY

Nothing happened, he says. Some operator you got yourself there, Charley. One more like him and we'll all be wearing striped pajamas.

TERRY

(turning to Charley for help)

It was a big nothing! The *Father* did all the talking.

JOHNNY

Oh, he did. Half an hour later a certain Timothy J. Nolan went into secret session with the Commission and *he* did all the talking.

TERRY

You mean Kayo Nolan, the oldtimer? He doesn't know much.

JOHNNY

He don't, huh?

(produces a bound folder of testimony from his pocket and slams it on the fender)

Well, he knows thirty-nine pages worth of our operation.

TERRY

How'd you get that?

JOHNNY
(thumbing "upstairs")
I got it. Hot off the press.

CHARLEY
The complete works of Timothy J. Nolan.

TERRY
Nolan? I knew he had guts but—

JOHNNY
Guts! A crummy pigeon who's looking to get his neck wrung!
(to Charley)
You should have known better than to trust this punched-out brother of yours. He was all right hanging around for laughs. But this is business. I don't like goof-offs messing in our business.

TERRY
Now just a minute, I—

CHARLEY
(suddenly)
What the hell are you doing with his sister?
(then turning to Johnny)
It's that girl, Johnny, the little Doyle broad has him out on his feet. An unhealthy relationship.

SONNY
Definitely!

JOHNNY
Don't see her no more. Unless you're both tired of living. Barney, you got her address?
(then to the others, businesslike)
Now listen, if we don't muzzle Nolan, we're into the biggest stink this town ever seen. We got the best muscle on the waterfront. The time to use it is now—pronto—if not sooner.
(to Terry, as he climbs in the car)
And you know where you're going? Back in the hold—no more cushy job in the loft. It's down the hold with the sweat gang till you learn your lesson.

Johnny twists Terry's cheek, but not in fun this time, as he has often done before. Now it is hard enough to draw blood. Then he turns to the driver.

Let's go!

The car drives off fast, almost running Terry down. He stands there looking after it, alone in the street, feeling his wounded cheek and then scowling as he looks down at the subpoena in his hand.

DISSOLVE

EXT FREIGHTER DAY

The ship is being unloaded. An empty pallet is swung from the pier and lowered into the open hatch by the up-and-down-fall tackle. Our CAMERA rides the pallet down into the hatch, to the second level, where Terry is working. A little removed from him are Pop, Moose and Nolan. They are unloading Irish whiskey.

NOLAN

(lifting a case onto the pallet joyously)

An Ir-rish ship loaded to the gunnels with foine Ir-rish whiskey!

He does a little jig and kisses the case as he sets it on the pallet. Pop and Moose laugh. But Terry looks over at Nolan tensely. Then he looks up out of the hatch.

EXT DOCK DAY

Johnny Friendly comes up to the edge of the dock with Sonny and Truck. Johnny mumbles something under his hand to Sonny and Sonny nods and jumps down onto the deck of the ship.

MEDIUM CLOSE ON DECK NEAR HATCH DAY

Sonny motions to Specs Donahue, glimpsed as Joey's killer at the opening. Specs nods and goes over to the winchman guiding the tackle over the hatch. He nods to him, and takes his place. Then he catches the eye of—

MEDIUM CLOSE BIG MAC

Standing on the deck just above the open hatch. A wordless message passes between him and Specs. Then he looks down into the hatch.

INT HATCH DAY

Terry works grimly, glancing up anxiously at Nolan, Pop and Moose whose mood, in contrast, is a whiskey-inspired euphoria.

POP

You see, Kayo, the good Lord watches over us after all.

NOLAN

(in an undertone, gaily)

When we knock off let's have a bit of a party. We'll drink to God and Ireland, its whiskey and its women, to Joey and Edie—and death to tyrants everywhere. . . !

As he finishes this he reveals surreptitiously the neck of a whiskey bottle concealed in his deep-pocketed jacket.

POP

(with mock concern)

You think one bottle's enough for all them toasts?

NOLAN

(grins)

Patrick, me lad, I'm ahead of you.

With a wink he reaches into his other pocket and draws up the neck of another bottle.

I was afraid one bottle might get lonely by itself.

(reaching into still another pocket and revealing still more bottles)

Now you see the advantage of a little man in a big coat.

POP

(laughing)

Definitely! Nolan, my boy, you're a walkin' distillery.

NOLAN

I wonder how many Hail Marys the Father'll make me say at confession.

(reflects)

It'll be worth it!

The pallet is loaded now. Terry turns and approaches Nolan.

TERRY

(with a nervous glance upward)

Listen—Nolan—

NOLAN

(backing away suspiciously)

What are you down here for—to see we don't make off with any of Mister Friendly's precious cargo?

TERRY
(miserably)
Nolan. . . .

MEDIUM CLOSE BIG MAC
Looking down into the hatch. Above him we can see Specs at the winch controls.

BIG MAC
Come on, Kayo, get it up!

INT HATCH DAY
Nolan and Pop look up at him and then back to their work with mischievous resentment.

BIG MAC
(continuing to bellow)
And don't be walking off with any of that. You know how the boss feels about individual pilferage.

INT HATCH DAY

NOLAN

(pretending to clean out his ears)

Talk louder. I can't hear you.

BIG MAC

If you kept your ears wide open instead of your mouth—

NOLAN

(shouting back)

If I talk too loud it's the fault of the nuns.

BIG MAC

And what in blazes have the nuns got to do with it?

NOLAN

(lowers his voice and confides in the hatch gang)

When I was a mere spit of a lad on Ferry Street in Dublin the nuns used to say to me, 'Nolan, don't be swallowin' ye words like fishballs. When you got something to say—

(Now he shouts up at Big Mac.)

—Talk with your mouth wide open,' so if I'm loud don't blame me–it's the fault of the nuns!

Pop laughs, at Big Mac's expense. The laughter is infectious and sweeps the hatch. Moose lets go with his loud "haw haw." Everyone laughs except Terry, who watches in a cold sweat.

BIG MAC

(furiously, from above)

Come on, knock it off!

The men laugh even louder.

MOOSE

Haw haw—that's a good one, Kayo.

BIG MAC

(able to shout above their laughter)

Knock it off! Stand clear.

(to Specs, the winchman, above the hatch)

All right, take it away.

Big Mac looks at Specs, touches his cap in a signaling gesture and nods.

CLOSE ON SPECS AT WINCH ABOVE HATCH
He catches the signal. From below the laughter of the men can be heard O.S.

CLOSE ON CARGO SLING
Full of whiskey cases, from angle of Kayo Nolan, Pop, Terry, and others, watching it rise out of the hatch. The general laughter continues. Terry is stiff with fear.

CLOSE SHOT SPECS
Suddenly he appears to lose control of the winch, guiding the up-and-down fall.

CLOSE ON NOLAN
Standing in the middle of the hatch, looking up, as the cargo net begins to plunge downward. The general laughter stops. From farther back in the hold Terry cries:

TERRY
(horrified)
Nolan. . . !

And tries to pull him back out of danger. Too late. The overloaded cargo net crashes down on Nolan. Wood splinters—glass shatters—and whiskey sprays. Kayo Nolan is pinned under the broken pile of cases.

TOMMY
(shouting up)
Get a doctor.

POP
(hard, flat tone)
A doctor—he needs a priest.

QUICK DISSOLVE

INT HATCH DAY

CLOSE ON FATHER BARRY
He stands over the body of Kayo Nolan, which lies on the pallet and has been covered by a tarpaulin.

GROUP SHOT HATCH
Pop, Moose, Luke, and the others stand near him. On the deck around the hold some seventy-five longshoremen have gathered, including Big Mac. Others look down from the dock and the loft. Terry is in the same position we left him.

FATHER BARRY

(aroused)

I came down here to keep a promise. I gave Kayo my word that if he stood up to the mob I'd stand up with him all the way. Now Kayo Nolan is dead. He was one of those fellows who had the gift of getting up. But this time they fixed him good—unless it was an accident like Big Mac says.

Pop, Moose, and some of the others glare at Big Mac, who chews his tobacco sullenly. Some of the others snicker "accident."

FATHER BARRY

Some people think the Crucifixion only took place on Calvary. They better wise up. Taking Joey Doyle's life to stop him from testifying is a crucifixion—Dropping a sling on Kayo Nolan because he was ready to spill his guts tomorrow—that's a crucifixion. Every time the mob puts the crusher on a good man—tries to stop him from doing his duty as a citizen—it's a crucifixion.

CLOSE ON TERRY

Voice of Father Barry continues.

FATHER BARRY

And anybody who sits around and lets it happen, keeps silent about something he knows has happened—shares the guilt of it just as much as the Roman soldier who pierced the flesh of Our Lord to see if He was dead.

SHOT OF EDIE ON DOCK

Listening, moved. Terry has come up behind her and stands nearby. She notices him but barely reacts. He listens intently to the Father's words.

(NOTE: I am not indicating in detail the other necessary reactions—those of Pop, Moose, the Negro Luke, the watchful hostility of Sonny and Truck, the murderous arrogance of Johnny Friendly, and the sophisticated cynicism of Charley Malloy. But most important of all is the impression being made on Terry.)

CLOSE ON TRUCK

TRUCK

Go back to your church, Father.

INT HATCH DAY

FATHER BARRY

(looking up at Truck and pointing to the ship)

Boys, this is my church. If you don't think Christ is here on the waterfront, you got another guess coming. And who do you think He lines up with—

CLOSE ON SONNY

SONNY

Get off the dock, Father.

Sonny reaches for a box of rotten bananas on the dock and flings one down into the hatch.

CLOSE ON FATHER BARRY
The banana splatters him, but he ignores it.

BACK TO SONNY ON DOCK
Terry turns to him. Edie notices this and watches with approval.

TERRY

Do that again and I'll flatten you.

SONNY

What're you doing. Joining them—

TERRY

Let him finish.

SONNY

Johnny ain't going to like that, Terry.

TERRY

Let him finish.

Edie looks at him amazed. Terry catches her eye, and then looks down, embarrassed at his good deed. They both turn to watch Father Barry.

CLOSE SHOT CHARLEY
Near Johnny, watching Terry and then looking at Johnny apprehensively.

INT HATCH DAY

FATHER BARRY

Every morning when the hiring boss blows his whistle, Jesus stands alongside you in the shape-up.

More missiles fly, some hitting the Father, but he continues:

FATHER BARRY

He sees why some of you get picked and some of you get passed over. He sees the family men worrying about getting their rent and getting food in the house for the wife and kids. He sees them selling their souls to the mob for a day's pay.

CLOSE ON JOHNNY FRIENDLY

Nodding to Barney. Barney picks up an empty beer can and hurls it down into the hatch.

INT HATCH DAY

It strikes Father Barry and blood etches his forehead. Pop jumps forward and shakes his fist.

POP

By Christ, the next bum who throws something deals with me. I don't care if he's twice my size.

Some of the other longshoremen grumble approval.

FATHER BARRY

What does Christ think of the easy-money boys who do none of the work and take all of the gravy? What does He think of these fellows wearing hundred-and-fifty-dollar suits and diamond rings—on *your* union dues and *your* kickback money? How does He feel about bloodsuckers picking up a longshoreman's work tab and grabbing twenty percent interest at the end of a week?

CLOSE ON J.P.

J.P.

Never mind about that!

CLOSE OF SONNY ON DOCK
Scowling.

Terry, nearby, is increasingly moved by the Father's challenge.

FATHER BARRY

How does He, who spoke up without fear against evil, feel about your silence?

SONNY

Shut up about that!

He reaches for another rotten banana and is poised to throw it. Almost simultaneously, Terry throws a short hard right that flattens Sonny neatly. Edie is watching, a deeply felt gratitude in her eyes.

CLOSE ON JOHNNY FRIENDLY AND TRUCK
A little way off.

TRUCK

You see that?

Johnny presses his lips together but makes no sign.

CLOSE ON TERRY AND EDIE
She moves closer to him. He barely glances at her, then continues listening to Father Barry.

INT HATCH DAY

FATHER BARRY

You want to know what's wrong with our waterfront? It's love of a lousy buck. It's making love of a buck—the cushy job—more important than the love of man. It's forgetting that every fellow down here is your brother in Christ.

CLOSE ON POP MOOSE LUKE TERRY AND EDIE
As Father Barry's voice rises to a climax—

FATHER BARRY

But remember, fellows, Christ is always with you—Christ is in the shape-up, He's in the hatch—He's in the union hall—He's kneeling here beside Nolan—and He's saying with all of you—

CLOSE ON FATHER BARRY

FATHER BARRY

If you do it to the least of mine, you do it to me! What they did to Joey, what they did to Nolan, they're doing to you. And you. And YOU. And only you, with God's help, have the power to knock 'em off for good!

(turns to Nolan's corpse)

Okay, Kayo?

(then looks up and says, harshly)

Amen.

He makes the sign of the cross. Pop, Moose, Tommy, Luke, and the others do likewise. Big Mac and Specs, seeing the others, reluctantly follow suit. Then, disgruntled, Big Mac climbs up out of the hatch and bellows:

BIG MAC

All right, fellows—break it up! Let's go!

Strongly moved, the longshoremen glare at Big Mac and then silently start back to their places on the deck, in the hatches, on the dock, etc.

MOVING SHOT

The pallet rises out of the hatch with the body on it. Pop sits casually on the edge with Father Barry who, in pantomime, is cadging a cigarette.

CLOSE ON EDIE AND TERRY

Edie crosses herself. Then she looks at Terry. They look at each other and the feeling in both of them is of some terrible hunger beyond their control. For a moment it seems as if Terry must go to her, but instead he turns away, slowly, slowly, as if this were the most difficult thing he was ever asked to do. Edie looks after him and we feel that she will yield to impulse and call out to him. But she looks down instead, finally, and closes her eyes, imperceptibly trembling against desire.

Luke comes up to her, but she is lost in her own most private thoughts and does not see him. He carries Joey's jacket, the one Nolan has been wearing.

LUKE

Edie. . . .

(nudges her)

Edie—

EDIE

(startled)

Oh—Luke.

LUKE

(quietly)

Joey's jacket. I thought maybe Kayo 'd like you to have it back.

Edie looks at him, and takes it silently. She hugs it to her, whispers, "Thank you," and, in a kind of sleepwalking, starts toward the entrance of the pier. Luke watches her anxiously.

LUKE

Sure you're okay?

She nods and continues on alone.

QUICK DISSOLVE

EXT ROOFTOP NIGHT

At the pigeon coop near Terry's rooftop window. Under the window is the mattress he uses as outdoor sleeping quarters on hot summer nights. Terry is staring in at the pigeons, full of his own troubled, bestirring thoughts. Edie comes up behind him almost silently, carrying the jacket.

TERRY

(turning)

Edie!

EDIE

(holding the coat out to him)

I—I brought this for you, Terry. It was Joey's.

(her conscious self trying to conceal the real meaning)

Yours is coming out at the elbows.

TERRY

(close to her—and not really caring what he is saying)

I don't rate it.

EDIE

Go ahead, wear it.

From the pigeon coop comes the soft sound of pigeons cooing as if upset.

EDIE

(under her breath)

Pigeons. . . .

TERRY

There's a hawk around. They're scared tonight.

She looks up and huddles a little closer to him. Now he reaches out for her—groping with an unfamiliar inexorable emotion.

TERRY

Edie—I—I—never said this to a girl before, I never knew a girl worth trying to say it for, but you—you're. . . .

EDIE

(whispering and suddenly wiser than he)

I know . . . I know. . . .

He kisses her at last, with pent-up violence and hunger. The sound of a deep-throated ship's whistle rolls across the river but they do not hear it. There is a tremendous sense of release and relief as their mouths and bodies press together.

FADE OUT

FADE IN

INT CONFESSION BOOTH DAY

Terry waits in anguish for the shutter of the confessional to open. When it does, Father Barry is glimpsed from within.

TERRY

(blurting it out)

Father, help me, I've got blood on my hands.

Father Barry looks at him.

TERRY

Bless me, Father, for I have—

To Terry's amazement the shutter closes abruptly.

INT CHURCH OUTSIDE CONFESSION BOOTH DAY

As Father Barry steps out of the booth, Terry hurries from his side of the booth and clasps Father Barry's arms violently. Father Barry keeps on walking and Terry follows him.

TERRY

What's the matter? I've got something that's chokin' me. I've gotta get it out.

FATHER BARRY

Someone else c'n take your confession.

TERRY

(following him)

But you're the one I want to tell—what you said over Nolan—about keepin' silent when you know the score—I'm guilty—you hear me? I'm guilty. . . .

FATHER BARRY

(trying to move on)

I don't want to hear it in there.

TERRY

I don't get it!

FATHER BARRY

(rapidly)

Tell it to me in there and my lips are sealed. But if I dig it out myself I can use it where it'll do the most good.

TERRY

But you've got to listen to me.

FATHER BARRY

I'll find you a priest.

Father Barry starts off again. Terry follows him desperately, under a terrible compulsion to bare himself to Father Barry. He grabs the Father by the arm fiercely, half spinning him around.

TERRY

(with relief, as he gets it out)

Listen, it was me who set Joey Doyle up for the muggers.

Father Barry stops and stares at him, realizing Terry is ready at last.

FATHER BARRY

Come take a walk with me, kid, and give it to me straight. There's nothing I haven't heard.

They turn toward the exit of the church.

EXT LONG SHOT CHURCH

They enter the park, on rise overlooking the docks, Terry talking to him eagerly.

CLOSE SHOT TERRY AND FATHER BARRY

TERRY

(pouring it out)

—It started as a favor—for my brother—you know they'd ask me things and it's hard to say no—a *favor*—Who am I kiddin'? They call it a favor but it's do it or else. And this time the favor turned out to be helping them knock off Joey. I just thought they'd lean on him a little but—Last night with Edie I wanted to tell her only it—stuck in my throat. I guess I was scared of drivin' her away—and I love her, Father. She's the first thing I ever loved.

FATHER BARRY

(almost brusquely)

What are you going to do?

TERRY

About Edie?

FATHER BARRY

Edie. The Commission. Your subpoena. I know you got a subpoena.

TERRY

It's like carrying a monkey around on your back.

FATHER BARRY

(agreeing)

A question of who rides who.

TERRY

If I spill, my life won't be worth a nickel.

FATHER BARRY

How much is your soul worth if you don't?

TERRY

But it's my own brother they're askin' me to finger—and Johnny Friendly. His mother and my mother was first cousins. When I was this high he took me to the ball games. . . .

FATHER BARRY

(violently)

Ball games! Don't break my heart! I wouldn't care if he gave you a life pass to the Polo Grounds. So you got a brother. Well, let me tell you something you got some other brothers—and they're all getting the short end while your cousin Johnny gets mustard on his face at the Polo Grounds. If I was you—

(He catches himself and drops his voice.)

—Listen, I'm not asking you to do anything, Terry. It's your own conscience that's got to do the asking.

TERRY

Conscience. . . .

(shakes his head ruefully)

I didn't even know I had one until I met you and Edie . . . this conscience stuff can drive you nuts.

FATHER BARRY

(sharply)

Good luck.

TERRY

(waiting for someone to do it for him)

Is that all you've got to say to me, Father?

Father Barry looks off.

LONG SHOT PIER WALL DAY

Edie coming toward them in the distance.

MEDIUM CLOSE FATHER BARRY AND TERRY

FATHER BARRY

It's up to you. Just one more thing. You better tell Edie.

Terry turns in Edie's direction, reluctantly. He goes off toward her. Father Barry stands looking after him.

CLOSER SHOT EDIE AND TERRY AT BURNED PIERS DAY

TERRY

Edie . . . Edie. . . .

EDIE

(turning to him)

Terry, what's wrong?

TERRY

I've been sittin' in the church.

EDIE

You?

TERRY

(almost inarticulate)

Yeah, yeah, it's up to me, it's up to me—he says it's up to me.

EDIE

Who says?

TERRY

The Father. The Father.

He is trembling.

EDIE

Terry—what's happening to you?

TERRY

I just told the Father.

EDIE

Told him what?

TERRY

What I did to Joey.

EDIE

(whispered)

You. . . .

TERRY

(louder)

What I did to Joey.

EDIE

Don't tell me—don't tell me!

TERRY

(plunging in)

Edie—it's—

What he starts to say is drowned out by an immense, prolonged blast of the whistle from the departing ocean liner. Terry shouts his story out to Edie compulsively but we cannot hear it over the rasping sound of the whistle. Edie is horrified as she catches enough words to realize what Terry is trying to say. The whistle pauses a moment, giving us just enough time to hear Terry shout—

Didn't know—

Then the blast of the boat whistle drowns him out again. When it finally stops, Terry is finishing—

—but don't you see, Edie, I never thought they'd—

(then hysterically as he feels her turning away from him)

I don't know what to do, Edie, I don't know what to do! I swear to God I—

She looks at him, turns and strides off.

TERRY

(calling, desperately)

Edie . . . Edie . . . What'll I do, Edie, what'll I do?

She doesn't look back. Terry watches her go, with mounting anguish; then he lurches on in drunken confusion.

QUICK DISSOLVE

EXT ROOFTOP DAY

As Terry, still dazed, enters onto the roof, Jimmy Conners, in his Golden Warrior blazer, is exercising the pigeons. He sees Terry and runs up to him. Jimmy talks in a whisper.

JIMMY

Hey, Terry, guess who's here . . . that joker from the Commission. . . .

TERRY

Looking for me?

JIMMY

He's got his nerve, gum-shoeing around here after what you told him.

TERRY

(grabs Jimmy)

Jimmy, suppose I knew something, say a mug somebody put on somebody. . . .

(violent gesture illustrates what he means)

You think I should turn him in?

JIMMY

A cheese-eater! You're kidding!

TERRY

Yeah, I'm kidding, I'm kidding. You don't think I should turn him in. . . .

JIMMY

(gives him a look)

You was a Golden Warrior.

TERRY

Yeah—us Golden Warriors.

(grabs Jimmy)

You're a good kid, Jimmy, a good tough kid. We stick together, huh, kid?

JIMMY

You was our first Supreme Commander, Terry. Keep out of sight and I'll tell him you're out.

TERRY

But I ain't out. I'm in. I'm in. Who's lying to who?

ROOFTOP ANOTHER ANGLE

Terry walks over to where Glover is sitting, rubbing his feet.

TERRY

You looking for me?

GLOVER

Not exactly. Just thought I'd sit down and rest my dogs a minute.

(smiles and rubs his ankle)

You know the next investigation we get into I hope it's got buildings with elevators in them. This one has been nothing but climbing stairs. And when we hit the top floor the folks are usually out.

Jimmy gestures behind him as if to say "Get a load of this square."

TERRY

(distractedly)

I guess it's pretty tough work at that.

GLOVER

(casually)

Well, it'll be worth it if we can tell the waterfront story the way the people have a right to hear it. Don't you think?

Terry shrugs. Glover studies him.

Didn't I see you fight in the Garden one night three or four years ago? With a fellow called Wilson?

TERRY

(still preoccupied)

Wilson—yeah—yeah—I fought Wilson.

GLOVER

I thought you were going to take him that night, but—

TERRY

(This is the key that unlocks him.)

You want to know something—I would have taken Wilson—

GLOVER

I think you could have.

TERRY

If I licked him I would have had the title shot instead of him—boy, I was ready that night.

GLOVER

You sure looked it. Something go wrong?

Terry has been growing more and more animated but now he becomes sullen.

TERRY

Yeah. Johnny Friendly and my brother had other ideas.

GLOVER

Such as what?

TERRY

(suspiciously)

Listen, this ain't for publication.

GLOVER

(amused)

I'm just resting my feet.

TERRY

Remember the first round how I had him against the ropes, and—

GLOVER

I'll never forget it. I thought it was all over.

TERRY

Yeah. My own blood—and they sell me out for a lousy bet—I had it in me to hit the top and—

(sighs)

Boy, if I wanted to, the things I could tell you about them guys—

(then catches himself and pauses)

GLOVER

(expectantly)

Yeah?

Terry is silent.

GLOVER

(rises)

Well, I better get going. Hit those stairs again.

(turns casually)

Was that a looping right or an uppercut the first time you caught him?

TERRY

(insulted)

Looping right! I never swung wild. I was strictly a short puncher—hooks—over 'n under—

(pantomimes, with violent short breath-releases)

—whop-whop!

GLOVER

Really?

TERRY

Yeah, really!

As Glover reaches the door, Terry keeps following him.

TERRY

Where you going? I'll walk along with you.

GLOVER

(grins warmly)

Sure. . . .

Terry follows Glover out, continuing to pantomime punches.

Jimmy looks after them and frowns.

QUICK DISSOLVE

INT FRIENDLY BAR NIGHT

Back room.

It is set up as an informal kangaroo court. Jocko is pointing at Charley Malloy, who is on the hot seat. Johnny Friendly is the judge, flanked by Big Mac, Truck, Sonny, Barney, Specs, J.P. Morgan and others.

J.P.

I didn't hear them, boss, but I sure seen them, walking along and smiling like a pair of lovers.

Charley looks uncomfortable. He hasn't finished his drink.

JOHNNY

(watching him carefully)

Drink up, Charley. We're ahead of you.

CHARLEY

(disturbed)

I'm not thirsty.

JOHNNY

(drinking)

After what we been hearing about your brother, I thought your throat'd be kind of dry.

CHARLEY

So they're walking along and smiling. That doesn't mean he's going to talk. There's no evidence until he gives public testimony.

JOHNNY

Thanks for the legal advice, Charley. That's what we always kept you around for.

(smiles wisely)

JOHNNY

(continued)

Now how do we keep him from giving this testimony? Isn't that the—er—as you'd put it—main order of business?

CHARLEY

(nervously)

He was always a good kid. You know that.

BIG MAC

He's a bum. After all the days I give him in the loft—he's got no gratitude.

JOHNNY

(offended)

Please, Mac, I'm conducting *this*—

(nodding to Charley)

—investigation.

CHARLEY

This girl and the Father got their hooks in him so deep he doesn't know which end is up anymore.

JOHNNY

I ain't interested in his mental condition. All I want to know is, is he D 'n D or is he a canary?

CHARLEY

I wish I knew.

JOHNNY

So do I, Charley. For your sake.

CHARLEY

What do you want me to do, Johnny?

JOHNNY

Very simple. Just bring him to . . . that place we been using. Mac, you take care of the details. Call Gerry G. in if you think you need him.

CHARLEY

Gerry G!! You don't want to do that, Johnny! Sure the boy's outa line, but he's just a confused kid.

JOHNNY

Confused kid? First *he* crosses me in public and gets away with it and then the next joker, and pretty soon I'm just another fellow down here.

CHARLEY

(horrified)

Johnny, I can't do that. I can't do that, Johnny.

JOHNNY

(coldly)

Then don't.

CHARLEY

But my own kid bro—

JOHNNY

(cutting in)

This is for you to figure out. You can have it your way or you can have it his way.

(gestures with his palms up and his palms down)

But you can't have it both ways.

(turns to Sonny)

Am I right, Sonny?

SONNY

Definitely!

JOHNNY

(thumbing Charley to his feet)

Okay, on your horse, you deep thinker.

Charley rises reluctantly, his confident, springy manner now gone.

DISSOLVE

INT TAXICAB EVENING (N.Y. B.G)

Charley and Terry have just entered the cab.

TERRY

Gee, Charley, I'm sure glad you stopped by for me. I needed to talk to you. What's it they say about blood, it's—

(falters)

CHARLEY

(looking away coldly)

Thicker than water.

DRIVER

(gravel voice, without turning around)

Where to?

CHARLEY

Four thirty-seven River Street.

TERRY

River Street? I thought we was going to the Garden.

CHARLEY

I've got to cover a bet there on the way over. Anyway, it gives us a chance to talk.

TERRY

(good-naturedly)

Nothing ever stops you from talking, Charley.

CHARLEY

The grapevine says you picked up a subpoena.

TERRY

(Noncommittal, Sullen.)

That's right. . . .

CHARLEY

(watching for his reaction)

Of course the boys know you too well to mark you down for a cheese-eater.

TERRY

Mm—hmm.

CHARLEY

You know, the boys are getting rather interested in your future.

TERRY

Mm—hmmm.

CHARLEY

They feel you've been sort of left out of things, Terry. They think it's time you had a few little things going for you on the docks.

TERRY

A steady job and a few bucks extra, that's all I wanted.

CHARLEY

Sure, that's all right when you're a kid, but you'll be pushing thirty pretty soon, slugger. It's time you got some ambition.

TERRY

I always figured I'd live longer without it.

CHARLEY

Maybe.

Terry looks at him.

CHARLEY

There's a slot for a boss loader on the new pier we're opening up.

TERRY

(interested)

Boss loader!

CHARLEY

Ten cents a hundred pounds on everything that moves in and out. And you don't have to lift a finger. It'll be three-four hundred a week just for openers.

TERRY

And for all that dough I don't do nothin'?

CHARLEY

Absolutely nothing. You do nothing and you say nothing. You understand, don't you, kid?

TERRY

(struggling with an unfamiliar problem of conscience and loyalties)

Yeah—yeah—I guess I do—but there's a lot more to this whole thing than I thought, Charley.

CHARLEY

You don't mean you're thinking of testifying against—

(turns a thumb in toward himself)

TERRY

I don't know—I don't know! I tell you I ain't made up my mind yet. That's what I wanted to talk to you about.

CHARLEY

(patiently, as to a stubborn child)

Listen, Terry, these piers we handle through the local—you know what they're worth to us?

TERRY

I know. I know.

CHARLEY

Well, then, you know Cousin Johnny isn't going to jeopardize a setup like that for one rubber-lipped—

TERRY

(simultaneous)

Don't say that!

CHARLEY

(continuing)

—ex-tanker who's walking on his heels—?

TERRY

Don't say that!

CHARLEY

What the hell!!!

TERRY

I could have been better!

CHARLEY

Listen, that isn't the point.

TERRY

I could have been better!

CHARLEY

The point is—there isn't much time, kid.

There is a painful pause, as they appraise each other.

TERRY

(desperately)

I tell you, Charley, I haven't made up my mind!

CHARLEY

Make up your mind, kid, I beg you, before we get to four thirty-seven River. . . .

TERRY

(stunned)

Four thirty-seven—that isn't where Gerry G. . . ?

Charley nods solemnly. Terry grows more agitated.

TERRY

Charley . . . you wouldn't take me to Gerry G. . . ?

Charley continues looking at him. He does not deny it. They stare at each other for a moment. Then suddenly Terry starts out of the cab. Charley pulls a pistol. Terry is motionless, now, looking at Charley.

CHARLEY

Take the boss loading, kid. For God's sake. I don't want to hurt you.

TERRY

(hushed, gently guiding the gun down toward Charley's lap)

Charley . . . Charley . . . Wow. . . .

CHARLEY

(genuinely)

I wish I didn't have to do this, Terry.

Terry eyes him, beaten. Charley leans back and looks at Terry strangely. Terry raises his hands above his head, somewhat in the manner of a prizefighter mitting the crowd. The image nicks Charley's memory.

TERRY

(an accusing sigh)

Wow. . . .

CHARLEY

(gently)

What do you weigh these days, slugger?

TERRY

(shrugs)

—eighty-seven, eighty-eight. What's it to you?

CHARLEY

(nostalgically)

Gee, when you tipped one seventy-five you were beautiful. You should've been another Billy Conn. That skunk I got to manage you brought you along too fast.

TERRY

It wasn't him!

(years of abuse crying out in him)

It was you, Charley. You and Johnny. Like the night the two of youse come in the dressing room and says, 'Kid, this ain't your night—we're going for the price on Wilson.' *It ain't my night.* I'd of taken Wilson apart that night! I was ready—remember the early rounds throwing them combinations. So what happens—This bum Wilson he gets the title shot—outdoors in the ball park!—and what do I get—a couple of bucks and a one-way ticket to Palookaville.

(more and more aroused as he relives it)

It was you, Charley. You was my brother. You should of looked out for me. Instead of making me take them dives for the short-end money.

CHARLEY

(defensively)

I always had a bet down for you. You saw some money.

TERRY

(agonized)

See! You don't understand!

CHARLEY

I tried to keep you in good with Johnny.

TERRY

You don't understand! I could've been a contender. I could've had class and been somebody. Real class. Instead of a bum, let's face it, which is what I am. It was you, Charley.

Charley takes a long, fond look at Terry. Then he glances quickly out the window.

MEDIUM SHOT WATERFRONT NIGHT

From Charley's angle. A gloomy light reflects the street numbers—433—435—

INT CLOSE CAB ON CHARLEY AND TERRY NIGHT

TERRY

It was you, Charley. . . .

CHARLEY

(turning back to Terry, his tone suddenly changed)

Okay—I'll tell him I couldn't bring you in. Ten to one they won't believe it, but—go ahead, blow. Jump out, quick, and keep going . . . and God help you from here on in.

LONGER ANGLE CAB NIGHT

As Terry jumps out. A bus is just starting up a little further along the street.

EXT MEDIUM LONG SHOT RIVER STREET NIGHT
Running, Terry leaps onto the back of the moving bus.

INT CAB RIVER ST. NIGHT

CHARLEY
(to driver as he watches Terry go)
Now take me to the Garden.

Charley sinks back in his seat, his hand covering his face. The driver turns around, gives him a withering look, steps on the gas, and guns the car into—

EXT MEDIUM LONG SHOT RIVER STREET NIGHT
They have reached a garage, and now the car zooms through the entrance. We catch a glimpse of Truck, Sonny and Big Mac.

MEDIUM CLOSE SHOT EXT JOHNNY'S LIMOUSINE NIGHT
Johnny is watching from across the street.

MEDIUM CLOSE ON GARAGE DOOR NIGHT
Big Mac and Sonny pull the big black sliding door shut until the screen itself is blacked out. Inside there is the roaring sound of a motor racing.

QUICK DISSOLVE

INT EDIE'S BEDROOM NIGHT
Edie is in bed. There is a pounding on the door.

EDIE
(frightened)
Who is it?

INT HALLWAY OUTSIDE DOYLE DOOR NIGHT
Terry, in a wild state after his escape, is pounding on the door.

TERRY
Edie, it's me—let me in—it's me!

He pounds on the door even harder.

CLOSE ON EDIE
The pounding continues.

EDIE
(fiercely)
Stop it! Stop it! Get away from here!

VOICE OF TERRY
(muffled)
I've got to see you. Got to talk to you.

EDIE

Leave me alone. I want you to leave me alone!

ANGLE ON DOOR

The pounding grows louder. Suddenly there is the sound of the door being broken open. Edie draws back against the head of her bed, pulling the covers around her. Terry runs in wild-eyed.

TERRY

I had to, Edie. I had to see you.

EDIE

Lucky Pop isn't home, he'd kill you.

TERRY

You think I stink, don't you? You think I stink for what I told you?

EDIE

I don't want to talk about it. I want you to go.

TERRY

(grabbing her)

Edie, listen to me! I want you to believe me. I want to be with you.

EDIE

(wrenching herself free)

How can you be with Charley and Johnny Friendly and still be with me? Either way it's a lie. It's like there were two different people inside of you. You've got to be one or the other.

TERRY

(in pain)

I don't want to hurt Charley—I don't want to hurt you. . . .

EDIE

It's you who's being hurt. By keeping it inside you, like a poison. Sooner or later it's got to come out.

TERRY

I know what you want me to do!

EDIE

I don't want you to do anything. Let your conscience tell you what to do.

TERRY

(pounding his fist on the bed)

That—

(pound! pound!)

—word again! Why do you keep saying conscience, conscience. . . .

EDIE

I never mentioned the word before.

In his agony he grips a glass standing on the night table.

TERRY

I keep hearing it and I don't know what to do . . . I don't know what to do. . . .

Without realizing what he is doing, he squeezes the glass in his powerful fist until it breaks. The glass cuts his hand. He draws back in pain.

TERRY

My hand.

EDIE

It's just a scratch. You won't die.

She turns away from him.

TERRY

Edie. . . .

EDIE

Get away from me.

TERRY

Edie, I need you to love me. Tell me you love me.

EDIE

I didn't say I didn't love you. I said *stay away from me.*

TERRY

(groping for her)

Edie, Edie, I—

His arms move around her. Her reaction is convulsive. Her hands move over him in anger and love.

EDIE

Stay away from me.

(her face close to his)

Stay away from me—

(closer)

Stay—

They kiss, lying across the bed, and the fever seizes them again.

—away from me!

Then, after some moments, they are distracted by—

VOICE FROM THE STREET

Hey, Terry, come on down. I got something to show you, Terry.

Startled, they cling to each other. The voice calls again—

Hey, Terry, your brother's down here.

TERRY

(more curious)

Charley?

VOICE

Charley's waitin' for ya. Come on down and see him.

EDIE

(whispers)

Don't go. Don't go.

TERRY

But Charley—maybe Charley needs me. I better see what he wants.

He goes.

EDIE

(calling after him)

Terry. . . .

She rises and calls toward the door—

Terry. . . .

Then she runs to the window.

EXT EDIE AT WINDOW NIGHT

EDIE

(calling)

Terry. . . .

WOMAN' VOICE

(O.S.)

You hear what I heard?

Edie looks up and to one side.

CLOSE ON MRS. COLLINS

Looking out another window of the tenement.

MRS. COLLINS

That's the same way they called Andy out the night I lost him.

CLOSE ON EDIE AT WINDOW

Horrified. Looking for Terry. She runs from the window.

CLOSE ON FIRE ESCAPE NIGHT

As Edie runs out onto it. She looks down wildly, searching for Terry.

A ship's whistle makes a mournful sound. A great luxury liner is heading out the harbor. Fog is drifting in over the roof. She peers down but can see nothing. She hears a wild shriek from the street and runs to the railing again. It is only a teenager whooping it up below. Then she hears shots—Bang—Bang—Bang—and the sound of a police siren. She raises her hands to her head and cries.

EDIE

Terry.

Then she hears the follow-up of the police siren. It is only a TV seat near the open window of the floor below.

TV ANNOUNCER

And now for your weekly dramatic thrill straight from the files of the City's Finest—*Police Patrol*. . . .

("Dragnet"-type music)

Edie turns away in exasperation. She calls down the fire escape into the fog.

EDIE

Terry!

There is no answer. Mrs. Collins appears on the fire escape in her kimono.

MRS. COLLINS

Don't go down!

Mrs. Collins tries to restrain her but Edie wrenches away—

EDIE

Terry!

She starts to run hysterically down the fire escape.

EXT LANDING UNDER FIRE ESCAPE NIGHT

As Edie is coming down the outside metal steps, Mutt is wandering along singing mournfully—

MUTT

Tippi-tippi-tin, tippi-Tin. . . .

A window opens and an angry voice cries:

LOUD VOICE

Drop dead!

An old shoe is hurled at Mutt, just as Edie turns toward him.

MUTT

(to the angry window)

Spit on me, curse me and stone me, but I suffer for your sins. . . .

LOUD VOICE

Go suffer somewhere else, you bum.

The window bangs shut. Mutt sees Edie and turns his attention to her.

MUTT

(calling to her in a crazed evangelical voice)

I seen it.

MUTT

I seen them put him to death! I heard him cry out.

EDIE

(impatiently—almost hysterically)

Who. Who did you see?

MUTT

His executioners. They was stabbing him in his side. And his soft eyes was looking down at them.

EDIE

(desperately)

Tell me *who*.

MUTT

(lifting his head from his hands)

Our Lord Jesus. When He died to save us. . . .

He gropes toward her as if to paw her.

EDIE

(with loathing)

Oh get away—get away!

She runs on. Mutt goes staggering off in the opposite direction, singing his song.

Edie runs on until she sees Terry in the mist.

EDIE

Terry!

She runs into his arms.

EDIE

(continued)

Terry, I'm frightened. More and more frightened.

TERRY

I'm looking for Charley. I heard Charley was waiting for me.

(calls)

Charley?

There is no answer. Terry frowns. Edie points through the darkness.

SAME VOICE IN FOG

Wanna see Charley? He's over here.

TERRY

(as they hurry forward)

Hey, Charley. . . .

EXT MEDIUM CLOSE WHITE WALL NIGHT

The headlights of a car suddenly illuminate Charley against the wall. Charley is leaning against the lamp post, in a very casual attitude, looking as dapper as usual. Terry and Edie run to him. The car drives off.

TERRY

Looking for me, Charley?

Charley seems to study them silently. Terry nudges him.

TERRY

Hey, Charley.

Charley slides down the wall and crumples to the ground. Dead. Edie screams. Terry drops beside the body.

TERRY

He's dead. He's dead. Those scummy, good-for-nuthin' butchers. . . .

The lights of an approaching car catch them in its beam. Terry reacts quickly, cowering against the wall and pulling Edie down behind him protectively.

TERRY

Behind me. Behind me. It may be them coming back!

They huddle in fear as the car comes closer; then it turns and the lights are no longer on them. Terry lets out a soft whistle of relief as the car drives off. Edie is completely panicked now.

EDIE

(in a horrified whisper)

Terry, let's go away.

Terry takes Charley's arm, which is twisted behind him, and straightens it tenderly.

TERRY

Charley.

EDIE

(hysterically)

I mean it, let's get away from here, first Joey then Nolan, now Charley—and any minute. . . .

(stares at him, almost saying "you.")

. . . I'm frightened—I'm frightened.

Terry seems not to hear. There are tears in his eyes but fury in his voice as he mutters to himself.

TERRY

I'll take it out of their skulls.

EDIE

I don't want to see you killed. I want to live with you. Live with you. Any place it's safe to walk the streets without. . . .

TERRY

(in a terrible mutter to himself)

I'll take it out of their skulls.

He rises, in a dangerous, animal rage.

EDIE

Terry, no, no. . . .

TERRY

Don't hang on to me. And don't follow me. Don't follow me.

(turns)

Call the Father. Ask him to take care of Charley for me. My brother. There's something I got to do.

He looks around, takes note of and strides toward—

MEDIUM SHOT PAWN SHOP NIGHT

A little way down the block. An iron grille protects the windows. Terry goes up to the grille and looks in. Edie follows him anxiously.

CLOSE SHOT PAWN SHOP WINDOW THROUGH GRILLE NIGHT

There are watches, rings, fishing rods, guitars, cameras, musical instruments, suits, furs, bowler hats, and—about two feet back from the window—a .45 revolver in a holster and a belt of cartridges.

TERRY

(muttering)

They put a hole in Charley. I'll put holes in them.

Edie sees what Terry is after and tries to restrain him.

EDIE

Terry, go home. There's nothing you can do now. It's locked up.

Terry looks at her unseeingly, then drives the toe of his shoe through the diamond-shaped opening in the grille, and through the glass behind it.

INT PAWN SHOP WINDOW NIGHT

Shooting toward Terry, the coveted revolver in the F.G. Terry's fingers cannot quite reach it. He has to press his shoulder painfully against the jagged glass in order to inch closer to it. He contorts his face in pain as the glass cuts through his jacket into his flesh. Blood begins to dampen his shoulder but with a final effort he gets his fingers around the gun.

EXT PAWN SHOP NIGHT

As Terry draws the gun from the window and slips it into his pocket, Edie sees the blood dripping from the rip in his jacket.

EDIE

Terry, you're bleeding.

TERRY

(in a flat tone)

Do what I told you. Take care of Charley.

EDIE

Terry, for God's sake.

TERRY

Get out of my way.

EDIE

No, I can't let you. I can't, you're—

She clings to him sobbing.

TERRY

(violently)

I don't want to hurt you, but—out of my way!

He flings her from him and goes on loading the gun, as she sobbingly watches him go off.

QUICK DISSOLVE

INT FRIENDLY BAR NIGHT
As Terry enters. The usual crowd are present: Barney, Specs, Sonny, Truck, J.P., etc. There is a comedian on TV and everyone is laughing but the laughter dies at the sight of Terry. He goes up to the bar tensely. Everyone watches in silence. There is a suggestion of men feeling for their guns but nobody moves.

TERRY
(to bartender)
Is Johnny in?

JOCKO
No.

TERRY
(suspiciously)
No?

To see for himself, Terry strides through to the back room and throws open the door. The back room is empty. Then he takes a seat at the bar so he can watch the room and the entrance. The customers eye him carefully.

TERRY

(to Jocko)

Give me a double.

JOCKO

Take it easy now, Terry.

TERRY

Keep the advice. Give me the whiskey.

Jocko sets the drink up. He notices the jagged tear in Terry's jacket and the spreading stain of blood from the shoulders.

JOCKO

What's wrong with your shoulder?

TERRY

(draining his glass)

Hit me again.

JOCKO

(in an undertone)

Listen, kid, why don't you go home before Johnny. . . .

Terry pushes his empty pony glass forward for another one.

TERRY

(sharply)

No advice. Just whiskey.

JOCKO

(pouring it)

Easy. Easy, boy.

ANOTHER ANGLE TOWARD ENTRANCE

Footsteps are heard outside the swinging doors. Terry turns to face the entrance, his hand going to the gun in his pocket. Sonny, Truck, Barney, and others all watch him, ready for the draw. Jocko automatically crosses himself and turns off the TV, which is now only an irritant. The swinging doors open, but it's not Johnny. Just a couple of happy waterfront barflies. But the moment they enter their grins vanish as they are made to feel the tension. They look at Terry, then they look at the goons watching Terry.

JOCKO

(to the newcomers)

What'll you have?

NEWCOMER

Thanks just the same.

The two men bolt out the doorway. In the silence we hear the creaking of the ancient swinging doors. The silence is oppressive. Terry works his hand over his bleeding shoulder.

JOCKO

You ought to go home and take care of that—

TERRY

(watching the doorway, growls)

First things first.

Once more steps are heard on the sidewalk outside the bar. Once more everyone is on edge for the showdown between Terry and Johnny. All eyes are on the swinging doors.

MEDIUM CLOSE SWINGING DOORS NIGHT

Father Barry enters, followed by Moose, Tommy, Luke. CAMERA goes with Father Barry as he walks right up to Terry.

FATHER BARRY

I want to see you, Terry.

TERRY

You got eyes. I'm right in front of you.

FATHER BARRY

Now don't give me a hard time.

TERRY

What do you want from me, Father.

FATHER BARRY

(putting out his hand)

Your gun.

TERRY

Mind your own business, Father.

FATHER BARRY

This is my business.

TERRY

Why don't you go and *chase* yourself?

FATHER BARRY

(slowly)

Give me that gun.

TERRY

You go to hell.

FATHER BARRY

(advancing)

What did you say?

TERRY

(just a trifle disconcerted)

You go to—

Father Barry throws a good right hand punch that catches Terry by surprise and knocks him down. Terry rises, feeling his shoulder, which is oozing blood now and weakening him. He charges Father Barry like a tormented animal.

Why you. . . .

Moose and Luke grab him, although Father Barry waits calmly.

TOMMY

(to Terry)

Get wise to yourself, you bum.

The word hits him. Terry drops his hands slowly, weaving as if weak from loss of blood.

TERRY

(chastened)

Take your hands off me. What you call me?

FATHER BARRY

(to Terry)

A *bum*. Look what you're doing. You want to be brave? Firing lead into another man's flesh isn't brave. Any bum who picks up a .45 in a pawn shop can be that brave. You want to hurt Johnny Friendly? You want to fix him for what he did to Charley—and a dozen men who were better than Charley? Don't fight him like a hoodlum down here in the jungle. That's just what he wants. He'll hit you in the head and plead self-defense. Fight him tomorrow in the courtroom—with the truth as you know it—Truth is the gun—Drop that thing and tell the truth—a more dangerous weapon than this little—

(reaches into Terry's pocket and removes the gun as he talks)

—cap pistol.

The two men look at each other. Father Barry's words cut him.

That is, if you've got the guts. If you haven't, you better hang on to this.

Father Barry offers the gun back to Terry contemptuously. Terry takes the gun, and holds it self-consciously.

FATHER BARRY

You want a beer?

(to Jocko)

Two beers.

Jocko sets them up and Father Barry and Terry drink them off, looking at each other. The drink seems to refresh Terry. He turns around to Jocko and slams the gun down on the bar.

Behind the bar is a large picture, in the place of honor, showing Johnny Friendly arm-in-arm with "Mr. Upstairs," beaming with self-confidence.

TERRY

Father, there is one thing I'd like to do.

So saying, he takes his revolver and hurls it into the face of the picture.

TERRY

(feeling better)

Tell Johnny I was here.

Terry looks around defiantly at the tense gunmen—and starts out with Father Barry and the group.

MEDIUM CLOSE JOCKO BEHIND BAR

Watching Terry leave. Breathing a sigh of relief as he picks up the gun.

JOCKO

(inadvertently)

. . . nice boy. . . .

Then he catches the dark looks of Sonny, Truck, Skins, Barney, etc., and busies himself at the bar.

FADE OUT

FADE IN

INT TRAVELING SHOT COURTROOM DAY

A courtroom door opens. It is the door out of which the witnesses are brought to testify for hearings of the Waterfront Crime Commission. A counsel is just finishing questioning Big Mac . . . We don't photograph this. We show Terry walking slowly towards his seat. Edie and Father Barry are in the audience. Also Johnny and some of the mob. We hear the dialogue (O.S.)

COUNSEL

(O.S.)

You mean to sit there and tell me that your local takes in sixty-five thousand, five hundred dollars every year and keeps no financial records?

BIG MAC

(O.S.)

Sure we keep records!

COUNSEL

(O.S.)

Well, where are they?

BIG MAC

(indignantly)

We was robbed last night, and we can't find no books.

CLOSER SHOT COUNSEL AND BIG MAC

COUNSEL

Doesn't it seem odd to you that five different waterfront locals were broken into last night and the only articles removed were financial records?

BIG MAC

(steadfastly)

What do you mean, *odd?* We was robbed like I told you.

COUNSEL

(waving him aside)

That's all. Next witness!

Big Mac steps down, mopping his brow. Terry steps up to the stand. They glare at each other as they pass. We CUT to Edie looking on anxiously from the spectators' section, to Father Barry, Pop, Moose, Tommy, and Luke sitting together leaning forward.

CLERK

Name?

TERRY

Terence Francis Malloy.

CLERK

Do you swear to tell the truth, the whole truth and nothing but the truth, so help you God?

There is a momentary pause.

CLOSE SHOT EDIE, FATHER BARRY

Sitting with Pop, Moose, Luke, and Tommy. Waiting for his answer.

CLOSE ON TERRY

His hand raised for the oath. When he answers, it seems more than a mere judicial formality.

TERRY

(firmly)

Right . . . *I do.*

COUNSEL

(rising)

Mr. Malloy, is it true that on the night Joey Doyle was found. . . .

CLOSE ON LARGE TV SET IN AN ELEGANT STUDY

We see Terry testifying on the TV screen.

COUNSEL

(continued)

. . . dead you were the last person to see him before he was pushed off the roof, and that you went immediately to the Friendly Bar where you expressed your feelings about the murder to Mr. Johnny Friendly?

TERRY

That's right.

During the above a butler's hand sets a highball glass down beside a rich leather chair, and a strong, manicured hand wearing an expensive ring picks up the glass.

VOICE OF BUTLER

Will there be anything else, sir?

VOICE OF "MR. UPSTAIRS"

(an impressive, heavy voice)

Yes, Sidney, if Mr. Friendly calls, I'm out, and you don't know when I'll be back.

VOICE OF BUTLER

Very good, sir.

The CAMERA moves in on the TV screen, the courtroom image spins, and when it finally stops, we are back to—

INT MEDIUM CLOSE COURTROOM ON TERRY DAY

COUNSEL

. . . Thank you, Mr. Malloy, you've done more than to break the case of Joey Doyle, you have held up a lamp of truth in the dark cave of waterfront crime. You may step down now.

As Terry steps down, he is quickly surrounded by police bodyguards, who lead him toward the chamber behind the courtroom. As he steps into the aisle Johnny Friendly leaps up from a long bench facing the aisle.

JOHNNY

(struggling to get at Terry)

You're a walkin' dead man! You're dead on this waterfront and every other waterfront from Boston to New Orleans. You won't go anywhere, drive a truck or a cab or push a

JOHNNY

(continued)

baggage rack without one of my guys having the eye on you. You just dug your own grave, dead man, go fall in it!

(spits in Terry's face)

Terry leaps at him instinctively. The gavel sounds repeatedly and there are cries of "Order! Order!"

Johnny wrestles with Terry, but they are roughly separated by courtroom guards who lead Terry off toward the door to the private chambers. Edie leaves her seat and tries to get to Terry but is kept off by the guards.

GUARD

Sorry, Miss, our orders is keep everybody away.

They lead Terry off, as the voice of the clerk is saying—

VOICE

(O.S.)

Next witness, Mr. Michael J. Skelly, also known as Johnny Friendly. . . .

DISSOLVE

INT CLOSE COURTHOUSE LOBBY AND STAIRS ON HEAVY FOOTSTEPS DAY

Terry's.

CLOSE ON TWO MORE PAIRS OF HEAVY FOOTSTEPS

Terry's police bodyguards.

MEDIUM CLOSE TERRY AND POLICEMEN CROSSING COURTHOUSE LOBBY DAY

Old men and bums are sitting on the park benches. Loitering outside are two of Terry's old chums, Chick and Jackie. Terry has to go right past them.

TERRY

(uncomfortably)

Hi Chick—Jackie. . . .

They look at him coldly, and turn away. Terry goes on, unhappily, the police guards just behind him.

TERRY

(half turning, irritably)

Have to walk right on top of me?

FIRST COP

Orders, Terry.

TERRY

You're stepping on my heels—you're making me nervous.

SECOND COP

Terry, you're hot, you know that, you should be glad we're this close to you.

TERRY

Trailing me like that, you make me feel like a canary.

FIRST COP

(grins a little)

Well?

TERRY

Now beat it—go ahead—beat it.

SECOND COP

Take it easy, Terry, take it easy.

He looks at his colleague and winks—they understand and fall back, allowing Terry to continue on down the stairs.

DISSOLVE

INT TERRY'S ROOM

Edie is preparing coffee on a little stove in the corner as Terry enters, drained and let down.

TERRY

Edie.

EDIE

I thought you might want some hot coffee.

TERRY

(shaking his head moodily)

Thanks just the same.

EDIE

Well, it's over.

TERRY

But I feel like—My friends won't talk to me.

EDIE

(bitingly)

Are you sure they're your friends?

Terry looks at her and then paces restlessly. He looks out and sees—

EXT ROOFTOP DAY
Jimmy, on the roof.

INT TERRY'S ROOM DAY

TERRY
(calling, halfheartedly)
Hey, Jimmy—how's the kid?
Jimmy doesn't answer. Terry goes to the window.
Hey, Jimmy!

EXT ROOFTOP DAY
Jimmy Conners, near the pigeon coop. He looks up at Terry sullenly and doesn't answer.

INT TERRY'S ROOM DAY
Terry draws back in defeat.

TERRY
Jimmy too.

JIMMY'S VOICE
(O.S.)
A pigeon for a pigeon. . . !
Through the open window is flung the body of a dead pigeon. It falls at Terry's feet. He looks down at it. Its neck has been wrung.

TERRY
(brokenly)
Swifty—my lead bird—
He looks out toward his coop—then climbs out the window and hurries toward it. We hold on Edie who watches him, worried, and then follows him.

EXT ROOFTOP DAY
Terry goes to his coop. On the floor are every one of his pigeons, perhaps three dozen, all with their necks wrung. Terry picks one up. Its head hangs limp.

TERRY
(looks off)
Jimmy. . .

EDIE
He's going to have to grow up too.

TERRY

(from deep inside him)

My pigeons. . . .

EDIE

Terry, you better stay in for a while. I'll come in and cook your meals. Be sure you keep the door locked.

TERRY

(not seeming to hear her)

Every one of 'em. . . .

EDIE

You heard what Johnny said. No part of the waterfront'll be safe for you now. Maybe inland—the Middle West somewhere—a job on a farm. . . .

TERRY

(mutters disgustedly)

Farm. . . .

He turns and starts back toward his room. She follows desperately.

EDIE

Does it have to be the waterfront! Pop, he's an old man, it's all he knows, but you—you could do lots of things, get into something new, anything as long as it's away from Johnny Friendly!

INT TERRY'S ROOM

Terry enters. Edie's voice follows him in as she trails behind him. He sits on the bed and looks at the cargo hook hung on a peg on the wall.

EDIE

Doesn't that make sense!

Terry doesn't answer. He takes the cargo hook from the wall and jabs it viciously into the floor.

EDIE

I don't think you're even listening to me!

He pulls the cargo hook out and jabs it into the floor again.

EDIE

. . .are you?

He looks up at her, frowns and then studies the cargo hook, tapping

it into his hand with pent-up feeling. The feeling is a strong and infectious one. Edie senses it and accuses him—

EDIE

You're going down there!

He looks up at her again for a moment and then works his hand over the handle of the hook.

EDIE

(her voice rising)

Just because Johnny warned you not to, you're going down there, aren't you?

He doesn't say anything but the determination in him seems to be constantly mounting.

EDIE

You think you've got to prove something to them, don't you? That you are not afraid of them and—you won't be satisfied until you walk right into their trap, will you?

His silence maddens her. She seems on the verge of striking him out of frustration and impotent rage. Her voice is hysterical—

EDIE

(continued)

Then go ahead—go ahead! Go down to the shape-up and get yourself killed, you stupid, pigheaded, son of a—

(struggles to control herself)

What are you trying to prove?

With a decisive gesture Terry takes the hook and sticks it through his belt. Then he goes to the wall and lifts Joey's windbreaker from the nail on which it has been hanging. He puts the windbreaker on in a deliberate way, and grins at her as he does so; then he walks to the door with a sense of dignity he has never had before.

TERRY

(quietly)

You always said I was a bum. Well—

(points to himself)

—not anymore. I'm going down to the dock. Don't worry, I'm not going to shoot anybody. I'm just going to get my rights.

(rubs the sleeve of the jacket)

Joey's jacket. It's time I start wearing it.

He goes.

QUICK DISSOLVE

EXT PIER SHAPE-UP MORNING

Big Mac facing the semicircle of several hundred men. Into this circle walks Terry. Other longshoremen instinctively move away from him as he approaches.

CLOSE BIG MAC

BIG MAC

I need fifteen gangs today. Everybody works!

He picks men out very quickly and they move forward from the mass.

MEDIUM CLOSE TERRY PIER DAY

He has taken his stand defiantly, with his hands in his pockets, looking Big Mac in the eye. Big Mac picks men all around Terry. He makes it obvious by reaching over Terry's shoulder to pick men behind him. Finally there are only a handful left around Terry, and then they are chosen. Terry is left standing there alone.

TERRY

(brazenly)

You're still a man short for that last hatch gang, Mac.

BIG MAC

(without looking at Terry, calls to Sonny)

Hey, Sonny, go across to the bar and pick up the first man you see.

Now Big Mac looks at Terry for the first time.

BIG MAC

Where are them cops of yours, stoolie? You're gonna need 'em.

He turns away. Terry stands there seething. He looks around at Pop, and the others ready to enter the pier. They look away, still fearful of Big Mac and the power of the mob, and feeling guilty for their passivity.

INT JOHNNY FRIENDLY'S OFFICE ON WHARF DAY

Johnny looks across at the isolated figure of Terry. Sonny, Truck, and Specs are with Johnny. On the desk are tabloids with headlines reading NAME JOHNNY FRIENDLY AS WATERFRONT MURDER BOSS. Under the banner head is a large picture of Johnny.

TRUCK

That ain't a bad picture of you, boss.

Johnny glares at him and pushes the paper aside angrily.

SONNY

I wish you'd let us go to work on that cheese-eater.

JOHNNY

(with both hands working)

After we get off the front page. Then he's mine. I want him.

EXT CLOSE PIER ENTRANCE ON TERRY AND BIG MAC DAY

As Sonny returns with "the first man he saw"—Mutt Murphy. Mutt and Terry glance at each other.

SONNY

Here's your man, Mac.

MAC

Okay.

Mac nods Mutt on into the pier, the one-armed derelict turning back with an apologetic gesture. Terry's fury grows. Mac growls at him—

You want more of the same? Come back tomorrow.

Terry looks at him, and then across at Johnny's office on the wharf. His hands begin to tremble.

He turns and starts walking slowly, resolutely, down the gangplank leading to Johnny's headquarters.

INT JOHNNY FRIENDLY'S OFFICE

SONNY

(seeing Terry through window)

He's comin' down!

JOHNNY

He's gotta be crazy!

TRUCK

(glancing out, growls)

Yeah, here comes the bum now. I'll top 'im off lovely.

Behind Johnny's back the click of a revolver safety latch is heard. Johnny whirls on him quickly.

JOHNNY

Gimme that.

TRUCK

(offended)

How are we gonna protect ourselves?

JOHNNY

Ever hear of the Sullivan Law? Carrying a gun without a permit? They'll be on us for anything now. The slightest infraction. Give.

(turns to the other goons)

All of you? Give—give—give—

Sonny, Truck and the others reluctantly give up their guns. Johnny turns to the safe and begins to open it.

JOHNNY

We're a law-abidin' union. Understand?

As he puts the guns in the safe and slams the safe door.

A law-abidin' union!

EXT UNION LOCAL OFFICE ON WHARF DAY

Terry walks compulsively down the ramp to the office.

TERRY

(shouts)

Hey, Friendly! Johnny Friendly, come out here!

Johnny comes out of his office followed by his goons.

JOHNNY

(shouts)

You want to know the trouble with you? You think it makes you a big man if you can give the answers.

TERRY

Listen, Johnny—

JOHNNY

Go on—beat it. Don't push your luck.

TERRY

You want to know somethin'—?

JOHNNY

I said beat it! At the right time I'll catch up with you. Be thinkin' about it.

As he starts to turn back into his office, Terry advances, steaming himself up.

TERRY

(louder)

You want to know something? Take the heater away and you're nothin'—take the good goods away, and the kickback and shakedown cabbage away and the pistoleros—

(indicating the others)

—away and you're a great big hunk of nothing—

(takes a deep breath as if relieved)

Your guts is all in your wallet and your trigger finger!

JOHNNY

(with fury)

Go on talkin'. You're talkin' yourself right into the river. Go on, go on. . . .

TERRY

(voice rising defiantly)

I'm glad what I done today, see? You give it to Joey, you give it to Nolan, you give it to Charley who was one of your own. You thought you was God Almighty instead of a cheap—conniving—good-for-nothing bum! So I'm glad what I done—you hear me?—glad what I done!

JOHNNY

(coldly)

You ratted on us, Terry.

TERRY

(aware of fellow longshoremen anxiously watching the duel)

From where you stand, maybe. But I'm standing over here now. I was rattin' on myself all them years and didn't know it, helpin' punks like you against people like Pop and Nolan an'. . . .

JOHNNY

(beckoning Terry with his hands, in a passion of hate)

Come on. I want you. You're mine. You're mine! Come on!

FIGHT ON UNION OFFICE DECK SERIES OF SHOTS

As Johnny takes an aggressive step forward, Terry runs down the ramp and hurls himself at him. They fight furiously on the deck of the houseboat. A fight to the death. A violent brawl with no holds barred. First one, then the other has the advantage. In B.G., longshoremen we know creep forward and watch in amazement.

LONGSHOREMEN WATCHING

LUKE

That kid fights like he useta!

Others nod but show no inclination to join in and face the goons.

BACK TO FIGHT

Which mounts in intensity as CAMERA FOLLOWS it around the narrow deck bordering the union office. Johnny knees Terry but

Terry retaliates with desperate combinations that begin to beat Johnny to the deck. Both of their faces are bloody and hideously swollen.

ANOTHER ANGLE GOONS
At this point Sonny, Truck and the other goons jump in to save their leader. Terry fights them off like a mad man, under vicious attack from all angles.

LONGSHOREMEN WATCHING
They'll kill 'im! It's a massacre! etc.
But they still hang back, intimidated by Johnny Friendly and his muscle.

TERRY FIGHTING
His face a bloody mask, being punched and kicked until he finally goes down. Goons are ready to finish the job when a battered Johnny Friendly mutters:

JOHNNY
That's enough. Let 'im lay there.
Terry is crumpled on the deck, senseless, in a pool of blood.

REVERSE ON EDIE AND FATHER BARRY
Pushing their way anxiously through the crowd of longshoremen.

FATHER BARRY
(tight-lipped)
What happened? What happened?

EDIE
(to young longshoreman)
Tommy, what happened?

POP
Where you goin'?

EDIE
(fiercely)
Let me by.

BACK TO TERRY
Blood seeping from many wounds as Father Barry and Edie run in and kneel at his side. Johnny Friendly near by.

JOHNNY
You want 'im? (as he goes) You can have 'im. The little rat's yours.

FATHER BARRY
(to longshoreman)
Get some fresh water.

EDIE
Terry. . . ?

FATHER BARRY
Terry . . . Terry. . . .

Terry groans, barely conscious.

ENTRANCE TO PIER ON BOSS STEVEDORE
In felt hat and business suit, symbols of executive authority.

BOSS STEVEDORE
Who's in charge here? We gotta get this ship going. It's costing us money.

The longshoremen hang back, glancing off toward the fallen Terry.

BOSS STEVEDORE
(waving them toward him)
Come on! Let's get goin'!

The men don't move.

BOSS STEVEDORE

I said—c'mon!

TOMMY

How about Terry? If he don't work, we don't work.

Others around him murmur agreement.

JOHNNY

(from B.G.)

Work! He can't even walk!

JOHNNY ON RAMP

Surrounded by longshoremen ignoring Stevedore's command, tries to drive them on.

JOHNNY

Come on! Get in there!

(grabbing Pop and shoving him forward)

Come on, you!

From force of habit, Pop begins to comply. Then he catches himself and turns on Johnny.

POP

(sounding more sad than angry)

All my life you pushed me around.

Suddenly he shoves Johnny off the ramp into the water scummy with oil slick and riverbank debris.

JOHNNY IN WATER

Cursing.

POP AND LONGSHOREMEN

Cheering Johnny Friendly's humiliation.

JOHNNY

(from water)

Come on, get me outa here!

BACK TO STEVEDORE

BOSS STEVEDORE

Let's go! Time is money!

MOOSE

You hoid 'im. Terry walk in, we walk in with 'im.

Others facing Stevedore mutter agreement.

TERRY FATHER BARRY AND EDIE

Terry's eyes flutter as they bathe his wounds.

EDIE

(to Father Barry)

They're waiting for him to walk in.

FATHER BARRY

You hear that, Terry?

(as Terry fails to respond)

Terry, did you hear that?

(trying to penetrate Terry's battered mind)

You lost the battle but you have a chance to win the war. All you gotta do is walk.

TERRY

(slowly coming to)

. . . walk?

FATHER BARRY

Johnny Friendly is layin' odds that you won't get up.

JOHNNY

(in B.G., shouts)

Come on, you guys!

Friendly's voice acts as a prod on Terry.

TERRY

(dazed)

Get me on my feet.

They make an effort to pick him up. He can barely stand. He looks around unseeingly.

TERRY

(continued)

Am I on my feet. . . ?

EDIE

Terry. . . ?

FATHER BARRY

You're on your feet. You can finish what you started.

Blood oozing from his wounds, Terry sways, uncomprehendingly.

FATHER BARRY

(continued)

You can!

TERRY

(mutters thru bloody lips)

I can? Okay. Okay. . . .

EDIE

(screams at Father Barry)

What are you trying to do?

ANGLE ON RAMP

As the groggy Terry starts up the ramp, Edie reaches out to him. Father Barry holds her back.

FATHER BARRY

Leave him alone. Take your hands off him—Leave him alone.

Staggering, moving painfully forward, Terry starts up the ramp. Edie's instinct is to help him but Father Barry, knowing the stakes of this symbolic act, holds her back. Terry stumbles, but steadies himself and moves forward as if driven on by Father Barry's will.

TERRY APPROACHING PIER ENTRANCE

As he staggers forward as if blinded, the longshoremen form a line on either side of him, awed by his courage, waiting to see if he'll make it. Terry keeps going.

REVERSE ANGLE BOSS STEVEDORE TERRY'S POV

Waiting at pier entrance as Terry approaches. Shot out of focus as Terry would see him through bloody haze.

TERRY

As the men who have formed a path for him watch intently, Terry staggers up until he is face to face with the Stevedore. He gathers himself as if to say, "I'm ready. Let's go!"

STEVEDORE

(calls officially)

All right—let's go to work!

As Terry goes past him into the pier, the men with a sense of inevitability fall in behind him.

JOHNNY FRIENDLY
Hurrying forward in a last desperate effort to stop the men from following Terry in.

JOHNNY

(screams)

Where you guys goin'? Wait a minute!

As they stream past him.

I'll be back! I'll be back! And I'll remember every last one of ya!

He points at them accusingly. But they keep following Terry into the pier.

WIDER ANGLE PIER ENTRANCE
As Father Barry and Edie look on, Stevedore blows his whistle for work to begin. Longshoremen by the hundreds march into the pier behind Terry like a conquering army. In the B.G. a frenzied Johnny Friendly is still screaming, "I'll be back! I'll be back!"

The threat, real as it is, is lost in the forward progress of Terry and the ragtail army of dock workers he now leads.

FADE OUT

THE END

Afterword

By Budd Schulberg

How *On the Waterfront* managed to reach the screen is a story with more ups and downs than the plot of the movie itself. Oddly enough, it has never been told. And yet it deserves its place in Hollywood film history as one of those rare moments when the writer succeeded—with massive help from his director/collaborator Elia Kazan—in getting his work to the screen despite the resistance of all the major studios, the Hollywood Establishment at its most stubbornly reactionary—or to put it more gently, blindly conservative—back in the fifties when studios could still be called "major."

Once upon a time—so our fairy tale fades in—this writer was living on his farm in Pennsylvania doing novels, and thinking he would devote the rest of his life to that nice, quiet work, when he received a visit from the famous director of *Gentleman's Agreement, Viva Zapata,* and *Streetcar Named Desire:* Elia Kazan. Kazan wanted to know if the writer would like to do a picture with him—not a Hollywood movie, but a film to be conceived, written, and shot in the East. Since I had just finished a novel and didn't feel ready to start another, the idea appealed to me. I felt I had left Hollywood as a place to live and work because the screenwriter was low man on the totem. Producers and directors used a writer's work but never seemed to respect him as the true source of the production. Even famous writers, be they Dorothy Parker, Scott Fitzgerald, Aldous Huxley, or John Van Druten, were treated as dispensable and expendable hired hands. Screenwriting, it seemed to me, was simply not a self-respecting line of work. Once in a while a Dudley Nichols enjoyed his work with John Ford, a Bob Riskin with Frank Capra, or a Ben Hecht would light up the screen for a month, make his twenty-five thousand, and get the hell back to "21." But until I got talking to Kazan about the possibilities of an "Eastern," I was quite prepared never to write another script for the rest of my life.

But if I worked with him, Kazan promised, instead of the Hollywood imbalance, he would respect the writer and his script as he had respected Arthur Miller, Tennessee Williams, and other playwrights with whom he had worked closely in the theater.

At first we discussed a film on "The Trenton Six," a northern version of the racist persecution of "The Scottsboro Boys." For a few weeks I researched the case in and around the grubby Trenton area. As Gadg (the familiar nickname for Kazan) and I sifted the complications of the Trenton case we came back to a subject we had touched on at our first meeting: the waterfront. The great harbor of New York—from the luxury line piers on the Hudson to the hoary docks of Brooklyn. Coincidentally, both of us had been bitten by the waterfront bug. A project Kazan had begun with Arthur Miller had aborted. I had been approached by a nephew of Harry Cohn to dramatize Malcolm Johnson's Pulitzer Prize-winning *Crime On The Waterfront,* but, ironically, the hard-mouthed Cohn would have none of it.

Now Kazan and I decided to plunge in again. The first step was research, not merely to read the soundly documented Johnson material but to go down to the docks and get the feel of it for myself. "To go down to the docks" is an oversimplification. What I actually had to do was work my way into what I soon discovered was a self-contained city-state: 750 miles of shoreline, with 1800 piers, handling ten thousand oceangoing ships a year, carrying over a million passengers a year and over thirty-five million tons of foreign cargo with a value of around eight billion dollars.

What I was soon to discover, following leads from Mike Johnson, was that this seagoing treasury was in the pocket of the mob—the Bowers mob on Manhattan's west side, the Anastasia family in Brooklyn (including "Albert A," chief executioner of Murder, Inc.), the Italian and Irish Mafia murdering each other for control of the Jersey waterfront. "Cockeye" Dunn (who later went to the chair) and his partner "Freddie McGurn" (who later retired in style to Miami) ran the Chelsea section on Manhattan's lower west side as if it were their private hunting and killing preserve.

At least 10 percent of everything that moved in and out of the harbor went into the pockets of these desperados. And if you were one of the 25,000 longshoremen looking for work, either you kicked back to a hiring boss appointed by mob overlords with the connivance of "legitimate" shipping and stevedore officials, or they starved you off the docks.

As inevitably happens under a system of oppression and vicious exploitation, a handful of braves were refusing to take this lying down. Such a group fascinated me when I met them with "the waterfront priest," Father John Corridan, at St. Xavier's in the dangerous Dunn-McGrath neighborhood. Father John's effect on me was nothing less than to revolutionize my attitude toward the Church. I approached it with the prejudice of a liberal freethinker. In Father John, a tall, fast-talking, chain-smoking, hardheaded, sometimes profane, Kerryman, I found the antidote to the stereotyped Barry Fitzgerald-Bing Crosby "Fah-ther" so dear to Hollywood hearts. In west-side saloons I listened intently to Father John, whose speech was a unique blend of Hell's Kitchen, baseball slang, an encyclopaedic grasp of waterfront economics, and an attack on man's inhumanity to man based on the teachings of Christ as brought up to date in the Papal Encyclicals on the reconstruction of the social order.

When I told Kazan about my discovery, he had to see this cassocked phenomenon for himself. Father John was in great form that day. He was furious at "Spellman," as he called the Cardinal, for recommending Bill McCormack as a recipient of the highest honor a layman could receive in the Church. McCormack was the "Mister Big" of the waterfront, into sand and gravel, trucking, stevedoring, and virtually everything that moved in and out of New York. The I.L.A. president, Joe Ryan, was "his office boy." What upset Father John was that these waterfront powers not only condoned but fronted for and benefited from organized crime: "Sunday Catholics" who defied, in the words of Pius XI, "the clear principles of justice and Christian charity." "The damn Power House could clean this mess up in five minutes if it really read the riot act to those S.O.B.'s," Father John exploded. "But the whole trouble is, they see all that cabbage. So we gotta help the boys on the docks do the job, from the bottom up."

After that session, Kazan and I paused to catch our breath at a corner saloon. "Well, what do you think?" I said, as proud of Father John as if I had created him myself. "Are you sure he's a priest?" Gadg asked.

"My God, he's wearing a cassock—and we meet him in St. Xavier's."

"Maybe he's working there for the waterfront rebels in disguise. . . ."

"Gadg, you've been seeing too many movies . . . Hollywood movies!" We both laughed, overjoyed, excited. Father John *was* a priest, a ruddy-faced Irish version of one of those French worker-priests, and we both knew we had to write his character and his morality into our picture.

The research took a dramatic turn. One of Father John's most devoted disciples was little Arthur Browne, proud of the fact that he was one of the stand-up "insoigents" in the Chelsea local run by the fat cats and their "pistoleros." With his flattened nose, his cocky laugh, and his stringpiece vocabulary, Brownie reminded me of those tough little bantamweights who used to delight the New York boxing fans.

Brownie promised to take me in hand and "walk me through the waterfront," but first we had to work up a cover story. Even in the bars friendly to the "insoigents," his pals would wonder what he was doing with this obvious outsider. They would think "reporter" or "cop" and in either case Brownie (and I) would be in jeopardy. Since I knew boxing and co-managed a fighter, and since longshoremen are avid fight fans, Brownie would tell the curious that we had met at Stillman's gym, fallen into conversation about fighters and had simply drifted over to the west side to quench our "thoist." "I'll point out the various characters and shoot the breeze and you just listen 'n drink your beer."

It worked fine. We drank boilermakers, Brownie got a group talking, I listened and made mental notes as to how I could work the dialogue into the script. One night we worked our way from bar to bar until we were opposite Pier 18. A saturnine man in a grey suit was at the bar and somehow, on my fifth boilermaker, I forgot my usual role and asked the stranger what he did. Brownie grabbed me, and the next thing I knew we were running down the street toward our "home block."

"Jesus, Mary, n' Joseph, you wanna get us both killed? Y'know who that guy was? Another Albert A. He's topped more people 'n Cockeye Dunn. I'm gonna tell Father John you're fired! We need a smarter resoicher."

Then he gave that undefeated laugh of his. The cowboys had

flattened his nose, thrown him through a skylight, and even into the river unconscious. "Lucky it was winter and the cold water revived me!" I lived with this sawed-off Lazarus and his wife Anne in their coldwater flat. I sat at the kitchen table and wrote down lines I could never make up: "Ya know what we gotta get rid of—the highocracy! Wait'll I see that bum again—I'll top him off lovely." And for revenge: "I'll take it out of their skulls!"

Sometimes it seemed as if everybody I talked to on the waterfront said something usable. I had left Hollywood because there were too many collaborators. Here I was surrounded by them—and welcomed every one of them.

The research became a year-long experience that I shared with Kazan. Out of day-and-night talkfests at my farm and his house on 72nd Street, with his critical-minded wife, Molly, sometimes sitting in as catalyst—"a helpful pain-in-the-ass," one playwright described her—we thrashed out the characters, the story line, the theme. Involved in the rebel longshore movement and writing articles in their behalf in *The New York Times Magazine, The Saturday Evening Post* and *Commonweal,* I finished the screenplay in a high state of excitement. Kazan shared my enthusiasm for it. In fact, he went further, "It's one of the three best I ever had! And the other two were *Death of a Salesman* and *Streetcar Named Desire!*"

Owing Zanuck a picture at 20th Century-Fox, he had written Darryl a zippy "Here we come!" letter about the zinger of a script we had sent out to him. I was a little worried. We had chosen a tough subject. We had taken real characters and put them through a struggle that was still being waged. Was it too somber, too real for the Hollywood Dream Machine? Gadg tried to allay my fears. Zanuck wasn't your typical big studio rajah. No L. B. Mayer who only wanted to make happy family pictures. Had I forgotten the Zanuck who made *The Grapes of Wrath, How Green Was My Valley,* and the then-controversial *Gentleman's Agreement?* "Darryl will love it," Gadg kept assuring me on the long ride out on The Super Chief. It was a writer's dream trip, long lunches in the dining car, with my director exclaiming, "I don't think you realize how great this is!" and the writer saying with belly and ego stuffed, "No, Gadg, tell me how great it is. . . ," whereupon my Greek friend would go into what was becoming almost a religious litany . . . *"Salesman . . . Streetcar . . . Waterfront. . . ."*

It was the nicest trip to California I ever had, and I hoped it would never end. When we pulled in to the old Santa Fe station in downtown Los Angeles, there was no studio limousine to meet us. When I remarked on this omission, Kazan, the prosperous proletarian, snorted, "C'mon, Budd, who the hell needs a studio limo?—let's grab a cab."

In our suite at the Beverly Hills Hotel (where my mother had brought me in 1920 to get away from the sinful Alexandria), I noticed that there were no flowers. "Flowers!" Gadg exploded, "What are you—some kind of a fruitcake? Who the hell needs flowers?"

"We're in trouble," I said.

"F'christsake, stop worrying. We've got a gutty script. Darryl has guts. He's got to love it."

"I think he hates it," I said.

"Budd, we just got here. Give the man a break. He's running a big studio. Wait 'til he sees us."

But I had been raised in Hollywood. I knew the unspoken language. No limo and no roses, no loving welcome note, and no invitation to come down to Palm Springs for the big Sunday croquet match spelled big trouble.

After an anxious weekend of intense tennis and Polo Lounging, we called Darryl's office at 20th first thing Monday morning. Apparently Darryl was still on his croquet field. We should "stand by." His secretary would call us as soon as she could set up an appointment. "Darryl hates it," I said, "or he would have called us from Palm Springs to say hello."

"Let's not jump to conclusions," said a now slightly nervous Kazan. We waited through Monday morning and were finally summoned in the early afternoon. In the outer office was Bella Darvi, the latest European import. My Hollywood upbringing warned me which of us would be called in first. We put in perhaps another half hour while Miss Darvi was in conference with Darryl. Finally we were in the Mussolini-sized office of the fearless producer of *The Grapes of Wrath*.

"Know what I love about this business—there's always something new happening!" Zanuck greeted us. "First there weren't enough frames to a foot, so the picture flickered. Then they got smooth natural movement. Then sound. Talkies! And just when the public was getting tired of black and white talkies, in came color, Technicolor—and now Cinerama! Can you imagine *Prince Valiant* in Cinerama? All those beautiful broads in silky gowns practically on top of you! I tell you, this is an exciting business!"

Gadg and I were exchanging looks. Our picture, he had written Darryl, was to be *black-and-white,* just plain *flat* black-and-white.

"Darryl," Gadg asked, "have you read our script?"

Kazan has a voice developed in the theater, but Darryl did not seem to hear it. As he went on about *Prince Valiant* and the wonders of Cinerama, Gadg interrupted, louder: "Look, Darryl, we didn't come all the way from New York to talk about your effing *Prince Valiant.* What about *Waterfront?* Have you read Budd's script?"

There was a long pause. Darryl took a step backward. We pressed forward. It could have been a scene out of one of the gangster movies Darryl had made at Warners. "Yes, Darryl, what about it?" I echoed Gadg. Darryl kept edging back toward the security of his desk. We kept moving forward.

"Well . . . I read it and boys, I'm sorry, but I didn't like a single thing about it."

A stricken writer: "Not one thing?"

A furious director: "Not a single thing about it? Darryl, you gotta be kidding!" And Gadg recited his lexicon of the script's virtues: "It's unique—something different—it catches the whole spirit of the harbor—the way you caught the Okies in *Grapes.*"

"But the Okies came across like American pioneers." The mark of a tycoon is to have answers ready for any challenge. "Who's going to care about a lot of sweaty longshoremen?"

Sweaty longshoremen! I thought of Father John's gritty group: unsinkable Brownie, the heroes of Pier 45, Tony Mike in Hoboken . . . were they not waterfront Joads who would endure? But Darryl was rubbing salt in the wound: "I think what you've written is exactly what the American people don't want to see."

There were angry accusations about broken contracts and our "handshake deal" with the porous Spyrus Skouras who had made large promises and cooed, "Make it a beautiful love story."

We had been given an office in the directors' building and when we ran out of Darryl's throne room we could think of nothing better to do than to trash that office—turn over the desk, throw the chairs, hurl the telephone . . . When our rage was spent, a little, we decided to confiscate the typewriter, typing paper, and office supplies and retreat to our foxhole in the Beverly Hills Hotel.

"Don't worry, Budd. Screw Darryl. I'm still very hot in this town.

Every studio in town wants me to do a picture for them. Jack Warner—"

"Don't tell *me,* tell *him.* . . ."

I was feeling a little sore at Gadg. *His* Darryl Zanuck and all that brave bullshit about *Grapes of Wrath.* A few minutes later he had Jack Warner on the phone. "Hello, Jack, listen, baby (Gadg can do the Hollywood bit pretty well when he wants to)—I've got a great property for you—a powerful story—*Public Enemy–Chain Gang*–the kind you guys do better'n anybody else in town!" He told our story, crisply, vividly, and then I heard a lot of "Buts. . . ." "But it isn't just a labor story. . . . But it isn't downbeat and grim, it's got. . . . But there *is* a love story tied into the main plot. . . . But. . . ."

When Gadg hung up I knew we were dead at Warner Brothers. And a day later ditto at Paramount and MGM. A messenger picked it up at dawn to rush it over to Columbia and it seemed we had hardly finished breakfast when the script was back in our laps. Belay that. Make it *teeth.* We didn't have any laps. We were pacing up and down in our bathrobes, all day, all night. Friends called to ask us out to dinner at Chasen's but we felt too beaten-down to get dressed, or be seen. Anybody who's ever worked in Hollywood knows how tough it is to go out on the town a loser. In my hometown losing and leprosy are interchangeable.

The *Hollywood Reporter* drove the final nail into what seemed to be our coffin with an item in its gossip column explaining that all the studios in town were cold-shouldering our project because it dealt with waterfront radicals and was pretty communistic.

Gadg wondered if we could do it as a play. And to his everlasting credit, after every Hollywood studio had thumbed us down, this director commanding a $250,000 salary—if only he would direct what *they* wanted him to do—swore to me, "God damn it, I'm going to stick with this thing if I have to get a 16mm. Eyemo and shoot it myself on the docks."

Since 20th Century had shut off our expense account, I decided the better part of valor was to get the hell back to Bucks County and try it as a novel. Meanwhile, whether it was determination or just nervous energy, we kept banging away at the typewriter we had liberated from 20th. Despite our depression, we kept getting new ideas for scenes, tightening, sharpening, rewriting. We took turns at the typewriter. The floor was littered with paper balls of discarded pages. Romantics might describe the atmosphere as inspired. Realists would call it manic.

Occasionally our door would open for room service or a friend from Suicides Anonymous, just as the door directly across the corridor opened, offering us a glimpse of the international producer who fancied himself as "S. P. Eagle," whose square handle was Sam Spiegel. Spiegel had been in Berlin when Hitler came to power. He fled to Vienna, Paris, London, Mexico, New York and finally back to Hollywood, where he had been fired by Paul Bern in the late twenties. Spiegel had gone down as often as Primo Carnera. But he had gotten up more often. With his keen mind, courtly manners (to those he courted), and sybaritic tastes, he was a very special kind of Wandering Jew, a throwback to the days when pirates were heroes if they were *your* pirates. When he was up he was very *up* and when he was down he knew the Hollywood and Middle-European game of behaving even more successfully. He had been up with *The African Queen* but now he was down with *Melba,* a costly mistake no theater even wanted to book. But the way Sam was living it up you would have thought he was celebrating an Oscar winner. We saw beautiful ladies enter his suite and heard Sam's ingratiating "Darling!" Waiters arrived with buckets of champagne. Sharon Douglas. George Stevens. If ever anyone knew how to ride out a loser, it was S. P. Eagle.

Enter Mr. S. In his elegant suit of midnight blue, smelling of expensively crushed French lilacs, he looked around in disdain at our paper-littered floor, our unpressed bathrobes, our unshaven faces, and urged us to clean ourselves up and come across the corridor to his party.

"Thanks, Sam, but we're in no mood for parties."

S. P. stared at the crumpled paper. "Are you boys in trouble?"

We each grabbed him by an arm and poured out our Hollywood horror story.

He looked at Kazan and became thoughtful. "Why don't you come to my room tomorrow morning and tell me the story?"

"It's got to be awful early," I said. "I'm flying home in the morning. Leaving the hotel at eight sharp."

"I'll see you at seven," said S. P. Eagle, and then, thinking ahead as always, "I'll leave the door unlocked so I won't have to get up."

Next morning on the dot of seven I walked through the party litter of the living room to the bedroom where S. P. Eagle lay inert in the splendid bed, as if in state.

"Sam?"

"Hmmm. . . ." Snores.

"Sam, it's seven o'clock, I'm here to tell you the story."

"Hmmm."

I didn't have much time before catching my plane so I began . . . haltingly, as it's not easy to talk into a cave of silence. But the muscle of the story began to stir me—damn it, there was a reason why Gadg and I had clung to it so desperately—and I began to pace around the large double bed ignoring its motionless occupant as I followed Terry Malloy through his waterfront ordeal. Occasionally I would pause and say, "Sam? . . . Sam?" receive a faintly reassuring "Hmmm" and press on. When I reached the climax, the eyes of the listener—with sheet and blanket drawn up over his chin—remained shut. There was a long silence, during which I thought about my waiting plane and the retreat to my Bucks County farm. Then there was a slight stirring under the blanket. The head managed to raise up a few inches. "I'll do it," a murmur rose from the pillow. "We'll make the picture."

Later that same morning I flew East with the Eagle who proceeded to set up a low-budget deal with United Artists. But there was still to be many a slip between script and production. Gadg sent our brainchild to Marlon Brando and he promptly sent it back. I claimed he hadn't bothered to read it. From my OSS days I had learned a sneaky trick of inserting tiny bits of paper between the pages of a book or manuscript. If they have not moved or fallen out, the work has not been read. The Brando script came back with paper slips in place. Then a tough little Hoboken kid agreed to play the part: Frank Sinatra. U. A. wouldn't put up more than $500,000 for Frank. Gadg felt we needed a minimum of eight. Then Spiegel and Kazan went to work on Marlon. Spieg wined, dined, wooed, and seduced. Gadg reminded him how he had fought to give him the lead in *Streetcar* when producer Irene Selznick preferred a bigger star, also very right for the role, John Garfield. Ironically I had talked to Julie—as we knew him—about possibly playing Terry Malloy when we were first getting into the research. But Julie's career and life were being destroyed by his pathetically "Un-American" activities, and he died of a heart attack before our project was under way. He would have been good, maybe great.

But as Gadg rightly insisted about Brando, he brought that extra something, the magic, the mystery, the gift of doing the unexpected that makes for genius.

With Brando on board, the wily S. P. was able to jettison Sinatra and U. A. and bring our project to Columbia who now accepted what they had twice rejected. We were in business at last. Kazan plunged enthusiastically into the casting, mostly from the Actor's Studio: Lee Cobb for the dock boss, Karl Malden for "Father John," Rod Steiger for Marlon's mobby brother, even the small parts, Marty Balsam as a waterfront crime investigator. For the innocent Catholic girl we thumbed through the entire *Players' Guide Directory* and finally came to Eva Marie Saint for her screen debut.

The screenplay that Gadg had fought for so uncompromisingly still went through a lot of rewrites. Spiegel was a taskmaster. A bear for structure. He thought it was overlength and sometimes discursive. Lots of times he was right. I respected his story mind. Still do. But he could be maddeningly manipulative. In his suite at the St. Regis, where our daily story conferences were held, I used to hate to go to the bathroom because I would return to the sitting room to find S. P. whispering to Gadg. I finally exploded. "I've been on this goddamned project for two years. I've taken practically nothing up front. I'm gambling like you on a percentage of the profits. It's beginning to break me. I've actually had to mortgage my farm. Sam hasn't even paid me the lousy five thousand dollars he's owed me for months. I've written my heart out on this goddamn thing. So what the hell can you two bastards be whispering about?"

I walked out. Gadg followed. We walked around the block. He was sympathetic. He didn't blame me for being sore. Sam did have maddening ways. He was naturally conspiratorial. He was jealous of the fact that Gadg and I worked so closely as a team. Just as he tried to separate me from Marlon or Marlon from Gadg. Divide and rule. He had to feel that he was in control. But, Gadg reminded me, there was one thing I should remember: with "S. P. Eagle" we were coming to bat with two outs at the bottom of the ninth. If we couldn't score with him, *Waterfront* was dead. "Let's face it, Sam Spiegel has saved our ass." I had to agree. Back to the St. Regis. The fight went on.

One tough round I won: the scene in the hold when Brownie—whom I called "Kayo"—is crushed in an "accident" and "Father Pete Barry," climbs down into the hold to deliver the last rites.

There he makes a fighting speech about "Christ in the shape-up," comparing the feisty "insoigent's" death to the Crucifixion. His dialogue—taken almost verbatim from Father Corridan's daring Sermon on the Docks—ran over three pages, and Spiegel insisted that while a speech that long might hold in a novel, it had no place in a screenplay for a picture that ought to be taut and spare. Day after day he hammered at this until, each time he asked me for the cuts in the Father Barry scene in the hold, rather than repeat myself, I would simply go to the window, open it, lean my elbows on the sill and stare out in silence.

At last, as he did so often, Gadg came to the rescue. "Sam, why don't we drop this and go on? I know it *reads* long but I know how to shoot it. Against all the tension between Kayo's pals and the mob. And Marlon caught in the middle, torn, feeling the guilt. I'll be cutting to him, and Tami Mauriello and Tony Galento (the fighters I had brought Gadg, along with Abe Simon, Lee Oma, and a lot of other old heavyweights to play the goons). It won't be static or talky, believe me. Let me handle it."

And finally when we got into production, in bitter winter on the Hoboken docks, Gadg handled that scene, and every other one in the script, with a fierce veracity that proved how effectively cinematic theatricality and cinematic verité can be combined in a unified dramatic experience. Often I would sit with Gadg late into the night while he mapped out his next day's shooting. He would point out what dialogue he thought was dispensable because of his visual attack on the scene. There were dawns when I sat with him on a frigid Hoboken rooftop, or in a squalid cold-water flat, or in the riverfront saloons that became "sets" for the picture, rewriting scenes that needed adjustments to fit the actual demands of those rugged locations.

At the outset Gadg had made his promise not to change a line of the script, but I would have to make a counter-promise: either to be on the set with him every day or to be on call to make the changes accommodating the practical and creative exigencies. Even though he had to shoot the picture in hostile territory, with police protection to guard him and the embattled company from an aroused waterfront underworld, Gadg kept his promise. Oh sure, lines overlapped, good, fresh words were thrown in spontaneously, but scene by scene Gadg stuck to the script, inventing and improving with staging that surprised and delighted me.

One day, fighting weather, fighting light, trying to hold together a crew so cold, miserable and contemptuously treated by S. P. Eagle that it was ready to mutiny, Gadg fell a day behind schedule. Sam came to the "set," a frozen, dingy alleyway, in his slick limousine with his compulsory accessory, a lovely lady. The scent of Chateaubriand from "21" was still on their breath. . . . Sam had called Charley Maguire, the heroic assistant director, at four in the morning to ask him "if he couldn't get Gadg to go faster." Although I had not been talking to Sam on the eve of the first day of shooting—when I said I would not show up unless he promised to stay away—we had made up one more time and he had also called me at some ungodly hour to urge me to urge Gadg to shoot faster.

Gadg walked away from Sam and came to me. "Budd, I've had it. I warned that son of a bitch, if he came on this set once more and broke our concentration, I was gonna quit!"

And now it was my turn to coo, "Gadg, one thing you've got to remember. We were down to our last out. Let's face it, Sam Spiegel saved our ass."

Gadg laughed, somehow finessed Sam and his lovely back into their limo and "21," and to on with the job he shot so brilliantly in thirty-five days.

When our picture went on to win its record number of Oscars, and break box-office records, revenge was more bitter than sweet. We kept hearing Darryl's deadly, "What you've written is exactly what the American people don't want to see." But just for once, getting a script to the screen in the spirit in which it had been conceived—thanks to that rare director who refused to make a distinction between playwright and screenplaywright—was victory enough. Find me a director who respects the *play*, as Kazan respected not only this one but Bill Inge's, Tennessee Williams's or Paul Osborn's, and the *auteur* theory will float away from the hollow, gaseous thing it is. What will remain will be solid screenplays, and solid directors who will not only embellish but vivify them.

Now—having been lucky enough to have a writer's champion calling "Action!"—a work that retains its hold on the public's imagination can be published for the first time in full, twenty-five years after Boris Kaufman's cameras first started turning on the Hoboken riverfront.

Textual Note

The copy-text for this edition of *On the Waterfront* is the "final shooting script" provided by Budd Schulberg. Spelling, punctuation, and obvious typing errors have been corrected; and the camera directions have been regularized. No substantive emendations have been made in the dialogue.

Budd Schulberg received the New York Critics Award, Screen Writers Guild Award, and Academy Awards for best story and best screenplay for *On the Waterfront*. Among his novels are *What Makes Sammy Run, The Harder They Fall,* and *The Disenchanted.* Other screenplays he has written include *A Face In The Crowd, Wind Across the Everglades,* and *Sanctuary V.*